Advance Praise for *Leadership Wisdom*

"Bob has brilliantly reminded us that leadership principles have remained unchanged since the dawn of man. This book has become my primary 'go-to' reference and is a must read for every student of leadership."

Richard Rierson, Executive Coach & Founder & host of Dose of Leadership Radio

"*Leadership Wisdom* is the first book I'll be giving to not only my wife, but my three, twenty-something-aged children as well–which says it all!"

Bryan Mattimore, author, *21 Days to a Big Idea*

"Drawn from the work of poets, philosophers and other sage thinkers, and refined by the tests and trials of practical executive experience, *Leadership Wisdom* provides a wealth of inspiration and insight into the arts of leadership."

Daniel J. Sweeney, Director, Institute for Enterprise Ethics, University of Denver

"Climb onto the magic carpet with leadership mentor Bob Vanourek and glide joyfully through eons of leadership wisdom. You'll become a more accomplished leader."

Bob Whipple, "The Trust Ambassador"

"The mystery and dignity of human leadership are beautifully captured by Bob Vanourek's selections from the world's great poetry and elegant prose and then elevated by his eloquent, personally candid commentaries. This is a treasury of leadership wisdom that all leaders should read annually. I certainly will."

Dr. Larry Donnithorne, author of *The West Point Way of Leadership*

"This century demands leaders who possess an impactful balance of authenticity and courage. This one-of-a-kind treasure surely provides a realistic moral compass to enable one to be authentic and courageous in the most challenging of times. This is a must for those executives I coach."

Charles Walsh, President, HOPS International LLC, International Center for Organizational and Leadership Excellence

"'Poetry is the breath and finer spirit of all knowledge.' So Wordsworth tells us, and so Bob Vanourek reminds us in this splendid book of classic quotations and the practical applications they provide for our lives. I know the quotations, and I've used at least 50 in my own life and work. Read. Learn. Be inspired. A wonderful book!"

John C. Bogle, Founder and former CEO, The Vanguard Group

"This book uniquely weaves together powerful leadership principles, life lessons drawn from wonderful excerpts in great literature and poetry, and Bob's inspiring life story. It is exceptionally valuable for leaders, followers, team members, parents, mentors, and coaches."

Michael J. Critelli, former Chairman and CEO, Pitney Bowes

"A powerful combination of the rich wisdom of the masters, an unflinching assessment of a high-powered career, and practical ideas for both the experienced and aspiring leader. I wish it had been written sooner."

Nancy Tuor Moore, Former CEO Kaiser Hill and board CH2M

"For those who seek to lead and make a difference in a clamorous world, leadership's exemplar, Bob Vanourek, is the North Star providing simple, powerful and timeless lessons to guide the way."

Walt Hampton, J.D., best-selling author of *Journeys on the Edge: Living a Life That Matters* and *The Power Principles of Time Mastery: Do Less, Make More, Have Fun*

"In a day when the road to leadership is often mistaken for the highway to celebrity, this book sets one on the path oft not taken, except by leaders willing to journey to that potent place heart and mind align."

Karl Bauer, Fire Chief and Executive Fire Officer,
Eagle River Fire Protection District

"Could the ongoing global crisis of trust be alleviated through a new leadership framework? Vanourek brilliantly combines timely and timeless lessons for current and future leaders, learned over his own career as a corporate CEO. Each story offers a leadership lesson and an opportunity for deep introspection on a new and better way forward."

Barbara Brooks Kimmel, CEO and Co-Founder,
Trust Across America Trust Around the World

"I love it. It is hard to say anything new in the well trampled literature of leadership, but Vanourek has come up with a brilliant idea that he has skillfully executed. After identifying some of the most memorable poems, writings and political speeches of our collective world culture, he has extracted from them nuggets of wisdom that can inform and inspire leaders of any generation. Building on his successful career as both student and practitioner of leadership, Vanourek proves to be a deft pilot as he guides us across a landscape that includes Robert Frost, Lewis Carroll, Shakespeare, the Bible, Abraham Lincoln, and Nelson Mandela. In his commentary on each reading, he converts their wise insights on the human condition into actionable principles that we can all benefit from in leadership and in life. This book is a *must* addition to anyone's leadership library. It is an engaging journey for all those who think deeply about how to inspire people and mobilize change."

Richard H. Chandler, Adjunct Professor,
University of California Irvine, and former CEO

"Brilliant. Vanourek's sensational new book provides a historical dimension to each of these classic poems and verses, exposing dimensions that lead to deeper, more enriching meanings. The real value comes from the 'practical applications,' challenging us to employ these timeless ideas to achieve greater results in today's turbulent world. A breakthrough in the clutter of leadership books."

Eric Chester, Author of *On Fire at Work: How Great Companies Ignite Passion in Their People Without Burning Them Out*

"In this elegant, meticulously researched, and well-crafted book, Bob Vanourek has captured the timeless wisdom of the world's great poets and novelists. What's more, he has applied this wisdom to the challenge of leadership, using his own deep experience to draw out lessons and immediate, practical takeaways. This is a heartfelt book that shuns the superficiality of many modern tomes on leadership to re-connect us with our core values and our underlying purpose. Thank you, Bob, for stepping into the arena once again and daring greatly!"

John Blakey, Vistage Chair & Speaker, Author, *The Trusted Executive*

"Take one part compendium of meaningful and memorable literature, add one part reflective memoir and useful self-help, stir, and bake. Bob Vanourek has cooked up a meal that is full of insight for anyone who wants to lead effectively and make a difference in the world."

Marty Linsky, Faculty, Harvard Kennedy School, co-author,
Leadership on the Line and *The Practice of Adaptive Leadership*

"A highly useful resource for leaders at all levels as they seek to hone their leadership behaviors. The selection of authors and use of personal examples provide an exceptionally useful learning resource. Especially valuable are the questions challenging the reader to deeply explore their individual leadership values and practices in their quest to become highly effective."

Sarah Smith Orr, former Executive Director, Kravis Leadership Institute and Visiting Professor, Claremont McKenna College and Adjunct Professor at The Drucker School, Claremont Graduate University

"A book of wisdom and profound leadership insights for passionate minds."

Richard Barrett, Author of *The New Leadership Paradigm*

"A much needed collection of wise lessons that inspire and encourage us to find our own wisdom, our own voice."

Richard Leider, Bestselling author of *The Power of Purpose, Life Reimagined, Work Reimagined,* and *Repacking Your Bag*

"Scripture declares there is nothing new under the sun, and Bob Vanourek's exceptional collection of the wisdom of the ages supports that notion. His commentary makes these insights relevant today by connecting them to twenty-first century leadership needs."

John Horan-Kates, Founder, Chairman, and CEO, Vail Leadership Institute

"*Leadership Wisdom* is just that. Wisdom. Presented in a thoughtful, creative way that makes it easy read to read in digestible bites. Bob's leadership experience resonates and adds depth."

Patricia Fripp, CSP, CPAE, Past President, National Speakers Association

"Terrific insights for leaders in our military and the public at large, now and in the future. A home run."

Jack Chain, General USAF, Ret., former Commander-in-Chief, Strategic Air Command

LEADERSHIP WISDOM:

LESSONS FROM POETRY, PROSE, AND CURIOUS VERSE

BOB VANOUREK

Published by Motivational Press, Inc.
1777 Aurora Road
Melbourne, Florida, 32935

www.MotivationalPress.com

Manufactured in the United States of America.

ISBN: 978-1-62865-285-7

CONTENTS

This book is dedicated to my family, friends, and colleagues who have taught me so much and given such comfort and support, and who have enriched my life immeasurably over the years. You have my everlasting love and appreciation.

FOREWORD

This is an inspiring book.

This is an informative and practical book.

This is a book that raises more questions than it answers.

This is a book full of the author's personal reflections, which stimulates you to think deeply as well.

This book is an antidote to the hubris of know-it-all executives and authors.

This is a fast-read book; however, read it slowly, and savor it to the last drop.

This book will surprise you with its insights and simple truths.

This book is a treasure.

That's really all you need to know about why you should purchase this book and take the time to read it.

You don't have to know Bob Vanourek personally to get his voice and perspective in this volume. Simply conjure an image of what you believe a wise person would look and sound like, and how this individual would share his or her insights with you. And, how that individual would spend the time with you because she or he cared about you and about what you needed to be your best self. That's the tone of this book-sagacious, warm, and considerate.

Bob has been an avid student of leadership his whole life. He spent thirty years primarily in the rough and tumble world of corporate turnarounds and strategic challenges. When Bob and his wife moved to Colorado, he began to teach, speak, and write about all he had learned about leadership, wishing to share the successes and failures he had experienced in order to help others not only learn how to lead better but to be better people.

Bob writes poignantly from his heart and is quick to give credit to many others for what he has learned; from extraordinary colleagues as well as the leadership experts he has met along the way. Bob is not only an experienced practitioner of both ancient and current models of leadership, but a deep thinker about what works, what doesn't, and what is changing as we move to confront the challenges of today and tomorrow.

Leadership Wisdom: Lessons from Poetry, Prose, and Curious Verse is different from any other leadership book you will read. It's not a chest-thumping recitation of all Bob has done as an award-winning CEO-indeed, he fesses up to many mistakes. Nor is it a fable about what some fictional character did to succeed; or a dense academic treatise on leadership principles. Nor it it a book of short pithy leadership quotes without any interpretation or practical applications.

Instead, Bob turns to the wisdom of the sages over the centuries and plumbs their insights from the poems and prose they have written. Then Bob offers his clear commentary on each passage along with some insightful practical applications based on his experience, challenging you to think about important issues regardless of where you are on your leadership journey. It's a powerful and perceptive approach.

You can read this book straight through, or just choose a passage or two each day to enhance your leadership skills. Bob quotes from over seventy celebrated authors and poets as well as political leaders, social activists, soldiers, educators, journalists, religious leaders from many faiths, and Native Americans.

If you are hungry for a better way to lead, if you want to experience the wisdom of the masters of literature, if you want to learn from an experienced and successful leader, then we are sure you will enjoy immensely this rich and unique work.

Jim Kouzes and Barry Posner, Co-authors, *The Leadership Challenge: How to Make Extraordinary Things Happen in Organizations* and *Learning Leadership: The Five Fundamentals for Becoming an Exemplary Leader*

INTRODUCTION

David Whyte is a contemporary poet who tells a moving story in his wonderful book, *The Heart Aroused: Poetry and the Preservation of the Soul in Corporate America*. He writes:

> As a poet, I did not foresee myself working in corporate America, a world I was taught to view with suspicion ... [the] telling moment of decision came on a visit to my local bank to get a construction loan for, of all things, a new writing studio. I knew the manager well from previous business, and he knew something of my work. He had always struck me as a cheerful and very vital man, but that morning he looked exhausted. His desk was filled from one corner to another with memos, notes, blinking phones, and piles of forms and loan applications. Greeting me, he looked as if he carried the weight of the world on his shoulders.
>
> Seemingly tired of this existence, he waved his arm vaguely over the array of pressing details and began to ask me questions about my work as a poet. After a brief tour of my travels, he asked if I was presently working on a book. "Well," I said, "I haven't written a word, but someone, for heaven's sake, wants me to write about the life of the soul in corporate America." There was a moment's pause, then he leaned across the desk, placed his hand on mine for the briefest of instants, and with the weariest and most soulful look I could imagine said, **"Tell me about it."** I looked at him, nodded back wearily and said nothing. Inside I felt something rise up; almost against my will, I heard myself saying, "Ask me like **that**, and I **will** tell you about it." (Emphasis added)

Like Whyte's banker, people hunger for words of wisdom about their lives and work. So many are burned out, struggling to survive, fighting their way through organizational bureaucracies, desperate to find better leaders, or ways they can lead themselves out of this morass.

Leadership expert James MacGregor Burns said, "Leadership is one of the most observed and least understood phenomena on earth." Many of us can cite a long list of atrocious leaders, but probably only a handful of great ones. Leadership has hundreds of definitions and scores of models. Frankly, leadership can be baffling. This confusion is why we have so many bad leaders today draining the joy out of our lives.

When I first read Lewis Carroll's poem "Jabberwocky" in college, I got hooked on poetry. It's in Carroll's 1871 novel *Through the Looking-Glass and What Alice Found There* and is replete with strange creatures and nonsense words. I memorized the poem and later recited it to our sons and grandchildren, on long runs to clear my mind, and on road-bike rides with friends to take our minds off the grind as we pedaled up a lung-burning mountain pass.

"Jabberwocky" is not just a whimsical set of curious verses. It also has a deeper meaning that is relevant to my lifelong passion: leadership. Over time, I have discovered many additional poems and prose passages that also offer deep leadership wisdom. The result is this book, which is not your typical leadership tome-we've got enough of those-and it's not just another collection of pithy leadership quotes. We'll dive much deeper than one-liners.

When I retired after thirty years in the business world, having led several publicly-traded companies and turnarounds as CEO, I had a chance to think even more deeply about leadership. I had a wonderful collaboration with our son, Gregg, in writing *Triple Crown Leadership: Building Excellent, Ethical, and Enduring Organizations.* I began teaching at the college and graduate level. I became certified as a leadership instructor by Harvard's Kennedy School and the Phi Theta Kappa Honor Society. Much of the Phi Theta Kappa curriculum is built around the use of classical literature from the Greeks through many contemporary authors. That's when I rediscovered the great wisdom in the prose and poetry I want to share with you here.

This book is my personal selection of poems, prose, speeches, and curious verses that convey for me some lasting leadership and life lessons. The elevated language and metaphoric images have touched me over the years. Of course, there are many interpretations of poetry and prose, and countless scholars have analyzed great works. I'm not a poetry scholar, so we won't be analyzing rhyming schemes, metrical patterns, or iambic pentameter. Instead, we shall focus on their content to distill leadership and life lessons, enjoying their ability to lift our spirits.

Even though many of the authors and poets I've quoted were not specifically addressing a leadership topic, I found a relevant leadership message in their words. My purpose is to draw out actionable and inspiring leadership lessons from these works, drawing also on my own leadership experience, touching on my successes, failures, and the muddy ground in between. Good leadership engages both sides of the brain and our hearts. As we progress, I'll exercise both your creative right brain with the verses as well as your logical left brain with commentary and practical applications, while hopefully touching your heart. My commentaries will describe what I believe good leadership to be.

Our opening storyteller, David Whyte, describes poetry as that "most intimate verbal art of human communication." Reacting to a draft of this book, a colleague, Laura Rose Forman, said "Good literature taps into the essence of human experience and transcends time."

The format of the book is deliberately designed with the left-facing page containing the verses, and the right-facing page containing some background on the author, my commentary, and some practical applications. Due to these space limitations on the left pages, I have used excerpts for some of the passages. In such cases, I hope you'll be stimulated enough to read the entire works.

Brief facts about the authors quoted or their passages are often cited based primarily on citations from the collaborators at Wikipedia, the crowd-sourced, online encyclopedia, which enjoys an average of more than 18 billion page views per month.[1] A 2014 study showed Wikipedia to have a 97.5 percent accuracy level.[2]

In the pages that follow, we'll hear from poets, presidents, prime ministers, political leaders, social activists, soldiers, educators, journalists, business leaders, the Bible, religious leaders from many faiths, Native Americans, a lyricist, and relatively unknown authors. Like all leaders, none of these authors is perfect. Being human, they all have flaws, and their lives, beliefs, or lifestyles can be criticized. But I find resonant and relevant leadership messages in the words they have written.

I have divided the book into three parts, even though several of the passages could easily apply to more than one theme:

- Part I Leading Yourself First
- Part II Leading Others
- Part III Leaving a Leadership Legacy

In the Final Reflections at the end, I'll describe good leadership in my own poem.

Appendix I recaptures the closing lines of each section providing you with a neat overview of the leadership wisdom from the masters I have quoted. Appendix II refers you to some other great works which I was not able to incorporate in this text.

I hope you'll appreciate the wisdom in these timeless works, that they will enhance your own leadership skills, and that you may live the full, rich, and joyful life you deserve.

Bob Vanourek

Cordillera, Colorado, February 2016

PART I

LEADING YOURSELF FIRST

"The mastery of the art of leadership comes with the mastery of the self…"

– Jim Kouzes and Barry Posner,
leadership experts and best-selling authors

I made a fateful decision at age twenty-four, a decision that would lead to many challenges, relocations, and some embarrassing pains in my life. A decision that would shape my destiny. It was a decision about leadership, but I didn't realize that at the time.

Somehow, some way, against all odds, I graduated with an MBA from Harvard. That was after four years as a scurrying-in-the-dining-halls scholarship student at Princeton, where I often worked double shifts to help pay my student bills.

I was stunned when the faculty at Harvard, based on my final grade point average, invited me to become a research assistant there and to pursue a PhD, which perhaps could lead to a faculty teaching position. Quite an unexpected honor for a scholarship kid from a lower-middle-class suburb of Chicago, whose parents never even dreamed of college. I had married my high school sweetheart, June, and we were living in student housing on hot dogs and beans from her salary as a legal secretary, driving our blue Volkswagen beetle around Cambridge.

I declined the invitation to pursue a PhD. I was desperately anxious to get out into the real world. I had one simple goal: "I want to run something." "Run" meant being in charge, in control, the boss. What did I want to run? Anything, as long as I was running it. Who was it all about? Me. What a presumptuous ego trip that was. Although, I wasn't aware of it at the time.

I was woefully unprepared to be a good leader then, and it took me decades to learn what I'm sharing in this book. Over a span of thirty years in the business world, I worked in eight different industries, and was privileged to be the CEO or president of five firms, from a start-up to two New York Stock Exchange firms that faced extreme challenges. I've been fired twice, painful and embarrassing experiences, so I can write as one who has been humbled and shell shocked.

I've also been hired and promoted dozens of times and achieved some award-winning successes with wonderful, talented colleagues from whom I have learned so much. One of the joys I have in life now is reminiscing with those colleagues about what we accomplished together, how we all grew as people, and grew as leaders through the crucibles we experienced.

The decision to forego a PhD at Harvard altered the course of my life. Over time, I became a leader with deep, practical experience while remaining a curious and lifelong student of leadership. To supplement my certifications to teach leadership, my son, Gregg, and I researched sixty-one organizations in eleven countries for our award-winning book, *Triple Crown Leadership*. Thus, I combine decades of leadership experience with academic credentials and solid research.

My hope is that you will learn from the leadership mistakes I confess to in this book, as well as from the successes I have enjoyed with my colleagues. I also fervently hope you will lead much better than I did in my early years. We need the next generation to do a better job than my generation has.

As I look back to my early days of leadership, I ask how I could presume to lead others when I hadn't yet learned how to lead myself? What was in control back then? My ego or my soul? My head or my heart? Did I listen more to the good in my inner voice, or was I seduced by control, power, and prestige?

These are the questions I can now answer clearly for myself, and they are the questions that many of you should also confront.

Do we who presume to lead have inner peace that radiates out to others, or are we a jumble of nervous energy, multi-tasking and moving frenetically through harried days? Do we take time to pause and reflect, finding some sanctuary to assess where we're going and how we're getting there? Or do we continue trying to run faster and faster? For me back then, it was always run, run, run.

Do we whine in the victim's role, or adjust our attitude and play the hand we're dealt to see if it can become a winner? Are we risk averse and indecisive? Or do we make bold commitments and take action, helping a few others, or maybe only just one other person? Do we persevere through difficult times, or give in easily? Do we rely on a higher power, whatever we conceive that higher power to be, for courage and comfort, or do we think we can do it all by ourselves?

Do we personally choose our paths in life, or do we passively follow the crowd? Do we stick to our core values and principles, or does our character (whatever that ethereal concept may be) blow with the direction of the wind?

Great wisdom to answer these fundamental questions of self-leadership is found in the poetry and prose written for us over centuries.

IF

RUDYARD KIPLING

If you can keep your head when all about you
Are losing theirs and blaming it on you,
If you can trust yourself when all men doubt you
But make allowance for their doubting too:
If you can wait and not be tired by waiting,
Or being lied about, don't deal in lies,
Or being hated, don't give way to hating,
And yet don't look too good, nor talk too wise:

If you can dream-and not make dreams your master,
If you can think-and not make thoughts your aim;
If you can meet with Triumph and Disaster
And treat those two impostors just the same;
If you can bear to hear the truth you've spoken
Twisted by knaves to make a trap for fools,
Or watch the things you gave your life to, broken,
And stoop and build 'em up with worn-out tools:

If you can make one heap of all your winnings
And risk it all on one turn of pitch-and-toss,
And lose, and start again at your beginnings
And never breathe a word about your loss;
If you can force your heart and nerve and sinew
To serve your turn long after they are gone,
And so hold on when there is nothing in you
Except the Will, which says to them: "Hold on!"

If you can talk with crowds and keep your virtue,
Or walk with Kings-nor lose the common touch,
If neither foes nor loving friends can hurt you,
If all men count with you, but none too much;
If you can fill the unforgiving minute
With sixty seconds' worth of distance run,
Yours is the Earth and everything that's in it,
And-which is more-you'll be a Man, my son!

THEME

ANSWERING CHARACTER QUESTIONS

Written in 1895 by Rudyard Kipling (1865–1936), winner of a British Nobel prize in literature, this poem is simply entitled "If." Kipling's conditions explore the depth and quality of one's character.

Character is made up of the sum of qualities that define a person: qualities such as trustworthiness, patience, commitment, kindness, willpower, work habits, resilience, humility, courage, compassion, empathy, honesty, responsibility, faithfulness, integrity, and more.

In the book *Courage: The Backbone of Leadership,* Gus Lee and Diane Elliott-Lee wrote,

Character is the result of sustained integrity and courage.

Perhaps a simpler definition of character is: who you are when no one is looking.

Kipling's character conditions are daunting challenges for us all. I would have great trouble never breathing a word after losing *everything* at a game of pitch and toss. Isn't a little bit of whining and moaning acceptable? At least for a short while?

Our character is not set in stone for any of us. Good character can be developed in people through the right parenting, leadership, reflection, lessons from our experiences, and mentoring.

Experience has taught me that people implicitly judge a leader on his or her perceived character. They wonder, "Can I trust this person? Does this person care about me, or only himself or herself? Is this person a leader of integrity?"

If people sense good character in a leader, then they will much more likely commit to and follow that person. If they have doubts about the leader's character, they may withhold their commitment.

PRACTICAL APPLICATIONS

1. Who is the real you when no one is looking?
2. Rate yourself on each of Kipling's conditions in "If" (there are thirteen).
3. If you scored well on each one, then you can be pleased with your leadership character.
4. For areas where you are lagging, what might you do to improve?

If strong character forms the basis of your leadership, you will have willing and committed followers.

THE MAN IN THE ARENA

THEODORE ROOSEVELT

It is not the critic who counts; not the man who points out how the strong man stumbles, or where the doer of deeds could have done them better. The credit belongs to the man who is actually in the arena, whose face is marred by dust and sweat and blood; who strives valiantly; who errs, who comes short again and again, because there is no effort without error and shortcoming; but who does actually strive to do the deeds; who knows great enthusiasms, the great devotions; who spends himself in a worthy cause; who at the best knows in the end the triumph of high achievement, and who at the worst, if he fails, at least fails while daring greatly, so that his place shall never be with those cold and timid souls who neither know victory nor defeat.

THEME

LEAPING INTO THE ARENA

These lines, commonly titled "The Man in the Arena," are excerpts from a speech by former U.S. president Theodore Roosevelt (1858–1919) delivered at the Sorbonne in Paris in 1910.

Leaders endure criticism. It comes with the territory. One needs a soft heart and thick skin to ward off the unfair blows that invariably come. During my tenure in the business world, much of the work I tackled was in turnarounds or organizations facing immense challenges. We encountered lawsuits in addition to outraged shareholders, customers, employees, and communities. Sometimes we found ourselves in the headlines, and employees suddenly left their company-logo ball caps and tee shirts in the closet, too embarrassed to wear them in public.

I *chose* leadership positions in companies facing challenges because I felt that if we could learn to lead better under duress, even extreme duress, then we could apply those lessons to less troubled situations. That's where I could leave at least some small mark on and positive contribution to our world.

Sometimes we made mistakes. Harkening back to Roosevelt's speech, his words speak to us about the inevitable errors and shortcomings of those who strive valiantly. Leaders fail, but at least they dare greatly. Roosevelt continued in his Sorbonne speech,

The poorest way to face life is with a sneer ...
To judge a man merely by success is an abhorrent wrong.

Teddy Roosevelt, arguably one of the greatest U.S. presidents, was a robust, daring leader. He believed it was better to try and to fail than to be one of those "cold and timid souls who know neither victory nor defeat."

PRACTICAL APPLICATIONS

1. Have you held back from some noble cause afraid to get into the arena?
2. Have you recently said, "That's not my job; it's not my responsibility"?
3. Have you been a sideline critic, sniping at those who ventured forth?
4. What would it take for you to overcome your fears, climb over the walls you yourself have built, and leap into the arena?

Leading well means having the courage to fight for worthy causes.

THE ALCHEMIST

PAULO COELHO

"What's the world's greatest lie?" the boy asked...

[Old man) "It's this: that at a certain point in our lives, we lose control of what's happening to us, and our lives become controlled by fate. That's the world's greatest lie."

...

The boy didn't know what a person's "destiny" was.

[Old man] "It's what you have always wanted to accomplish. Everyone, when they are young, knows what their destiny is.

At that point in their lives, everything is clear and everything is possible. They are not afraid to dream, and to yearn for everything they would like to see happen to them in their lives. But, as time passes, a mysterious force begins to convince them that it will be impossible for them to realize their destiny.... whoever you are, or whatever it is that you do, when you really want something, it's because that desire originated in the soul of the universe. It's your mission on earth."

...

"Why do we have to listen to our hearts?" the boy asked ...

[The alchemist] "Because, wherever your heart is, that is where you'll find your treasure."

...

[The alchemist] "Tell your heart that the fear of suffering is worse than the suffering itself. And that no heart has ever suffered when it goes in search of its dreams, because every second of the search is a second's encounter with God and with eternity."

THEME

FOLLOWING YOUR HEART

Paulo Coelho (1947–) is an award-winning, Brazilian lyricist and novelist. These passages are from his most famous novel, *The Alchemist,* published in 1988.

The Alchemist tells the magical story of an Andalusian shepherd boy, Santiago, who sets out on a quest to find a wonderful treasure. He travels from Spain to the markets of Tangiers and then into the Egyptian desert meeting wise guides and an alchemist (a mythical person who can turn a base metal into gold). The boy follows his dreams, learns to listen to his heart, and refuses to let his life be determined by forces outside his control.

Too often in life, we give up on our childhood dreams and feel that some unmovable fate controls us. Or, we fear the pain and suffering that we may encounter if we embark upon the quest to pursue our dreams. We stop listening to what's in our hearts, that echoing of the soul of the universe whispering to us about our true purpose in life.

Santiago travels far, risks his life, faces his fears bravely, and encounters wondrous sites and wise people. He meets the love of his life and finds his true treasure in the strangest of places.

So it is with all of us. To find our true purpose in life, we must connect with the soul of the universe by listening to what's in our hearts. We must risk venturing forth, leading ourselves through the fears and the dangers we'll encounter, and being open to exploration and adventure.

After June and I married, we set out on our own adventures. We met countless new friends and colleagues in the course of seventeen moves and the eleven states where we have lived. For me, it was also working in eight different industries and having the honor to lead five different companies. What an odyssey for us.

PRACTICAL APPLICATIONS

1. Do you feel controlled by fate?
2. Are you willing to break free and pursue your dreams?
3. What does your heart tell you your dreams are?
4. What can you start to do today to pursue your dreams and follow your heart?

Leading yourself well means pursuing the dream your heart whispers.

THE ROAD NOT TAKEN

ROBERT FROST

Two roads diverged in a yellow wood,
And sorry I could not travel both
And be one traveler, long I stood
And looked down one as far as I could
To where it bent in the undergrowth;

Then took the other, as just as fair,
And having perhaps the better claim,
Because it was grassy and wanted wear;
Though as for that the passing there
Had worn them really about the same,

And both that morning equally lay
In leaves no step had trodden black.
Oh, I kept the first for another day!
Yet knowing how way leads on to way,
I doubted if I should ever come back.

I shall be telling this with a sigh
Somewhere ages and ages hence:
Two roads diverged in a wood, and I–
I took the one less traveled by,
And that has made all the difference.

THEME

CHOOSING YOUR ROADS WISELY

Robert Frost (1874–1963) was a popular American poet, who won the Pulitzer Prize for Poetry an incredible four times. Published in 1916, "The Road Not Taken" has always intrigued me. Frost himself described it as a "tricky poem." He said it focused on indecision and on people finding meaning in inconsequential choices.[3] Frost's focus on indecision evokes for me Yogi Berra's quip, "If you come to a fork in the road, take it," an aphorism that encourages one to make a decision and not be baffled by choices.

One of the beauties of poetry is that readers are free to find their own meaning in the verses. I find another intriguing message in "The Road Not Taken" about making choices without realizing the *consequential* implications those choices sometimes have on our lives. I take my cue from the poem's last two lines:

I took the one less traveled by,
And that has made all the difference.

We choose a job, for example, in an industry in a certain location with a certain firm for reasons sometimes less than cogent: to be close to home, because that's where our friends are going, because it has the shortest commute, or the highest pay. We delude ourselves by saying, "If this job doesn't work out, I can always leave."

Perhaps it did not seem there was much of a difference between the paths we encountered when in fact the differences were vast. We might discover this company is not at all what we thought, or even what they promised. Corners are cut; values are compromised; people are disposable assets.

You regret the choice you made. But there are bills and a mortgage to pay, a family to support, and it's difficult to make a career change. It's better, then, just to stay put–stuck. And "knowing how way leads on to way," we never come back. What a consequential tragedy for the only life we have to lead.

Frost's traveler takes the road *less* traveled. He wisely chooses the path that's right for him, even if that direction is unconventional, and that makes "all the difference."

PRACTICAL APPLICATIONS

1. Has your life been on the well-trodden path everyone else has followed?
2. Is there another, not-yet-taken road that still beckons to you?
3. What would it take to venture down that road?
4. Make a list today of just how you could make that turn.
5. Consider how that turn may make *all the difference* in your life.

Leading your life well means being thoughtful about the roads you choose.

STOPPING BY WOODS ON A SNOWY EVENING

ROBERT FROST

Whose woods these are I think I know.
His house is in the village though;
He will not see me stopping here
To watch his woods fill up with snow.

My little horse must think it queer
To stop without a farmhouse near
Between the woods and frozen lake
The darkest evening of the year.

He gives his harness bells a shake
To ask if there is some mistake.
The only other sound's the sweep
Of easy wind and downy flake.

The woods are lovely, dark and deep,
But I have promises to keep,
And miles to go before I sleep,
And miles to go before I sleep.

THEME

PAUSING AND ACTING

Robert Frost wrote "Stopping by Woods on a Snowy Evening" in 1922. Frost was one of former U.S. President John F. Kennedy's favorite poets. When JFK's casket arrived at the White House after his assassination, Westinghouse broadcaster Sid Davis, overcome with grief and emotion, signed off his broadcast with a passage from this Frost poem.[4]

"Stopping by Woods on a Snowy Evening" is a seemingly simple poem, but several lines have always intrigued me. "The darkest evening of the year" might, of course, refer to a cloudy, moonless night at the winter solstice. But it might also refer to some ominous event that has transpired that demands the traveler's attention-perhaps what former U.S. President Franklin Roosevelt might have felt on the night of the attack on Pearl Harbor?

The driver in Frost's poem might long to linger in the "lovely, dark, and deep" woods, but he has "promises to keep, and miles to go before I sleep, and miles to go before I sleep." Why does Frost repeat these closing words? I sense the driver yearns for rest and sleep, but he knows he must carry on, even on this "darkest evening of the year," honoring the promises he has made.

Leaders don't take the easy way out. They don't procrastinate. They honor their promises, delivering on their commitments. If they can't complete their obligations, they come forth promptly, explain the circumstances that have caused the delay, and then affirm a new commitment.

Leaders should pause occasionally, lingering in their own lovely and snowy woods, drinking in the moonlight and stars, appreciating nature. But then they must move forward, making the tough decisions that leadership demands. Leaders act.

PRACTICAL APPLICATIONS

1. Are there some restful places you should visit more to quiet your churning mind?
2. What difficult tasks have you been putting off?
3. What might you begin to do today to honor your promises and keep your commitments?

When under extreme stress, good leaders pause to renew themselves, and then they act.

SLOW ME DOWN LORD

WILFERD PETERSON

Slow me down, Lord!
Ease the pounding of my heart
By the quieting of my mind.
Steady my harried pace
With a vision of the eternal reach of time.

Give me, amidst the confusions of my day,
The calmness of the everlasting hills.
Break the tensions of my nerves and muscles
With the music of the singing streams
Which live in my memory.

Help me to know
The magic restoring power of sleep,

Teach me the art of taking minute vacations
...
Of slowing down to look at a flower;
To chat with a friend,
To pat a dog;
To read a few lines from a good book.

Remind me each day
Of the fable of the hare and the tortoise,
That I may know that the race is not always to the swift;
That there is more to life
Than increasing its speed.

Let me look upward
Into the branches of the towering oak
And know that it grew great and strong
Because it grew slowly and well.

Slow me down, Lord,
And inspire me to send my roots deep
Into the soil of life's enduring values
That I may grow toward the stars
Of my greater destiny.

THEME

SLOWING DOWN

"Slow Me Down Lord" is a wonderfully popular poem, sometimes attributed to Orin L. Crain, an Oklahoma resident, who supposedly wrote it in 1957. Wikipedia attributes it to Wilferd Arlan Peterson (1900–1995), an American author who wrote "Words To Live By" for *This Week* magazine, a Sunday newspaper supplement.[5] Whoever its author was, the essence of the poem originates from the Middle East in a Hittite prayer written over 2,000 years ago.[6]

Too many of us get caught up in the frantic pace of today's world. Our minds are jumbled with all that must be done. I operated that way for too long. I remember sometimes scheduling meetings in ten or fifteen-minute blocks, or holding meetings standing up so we wouldn't get too comfortable. I remember a new job in a new state where I had to get a new driver's license, so I scheduled a meeting with colleagues while standing in the long, slow-moving line at the Motor Vehicle Department. People around us must have thought we were nuts.

I remember debating with my son, Gregg, about balance in life. I felt he didn't understand the commitment it took to be successful in life. Balance could come later. But Gregg was right and does a better job with work/life integration and balance than I did.

Sometimes there is no "later" for balance or enjoying life. Sometimes the pace becomes so addictive you don't realize what's happening to your soul and how you affect those around you. Like the endorphin highs I got from distance running, my work pace became addictive. When I left my last CEO job and retired to the Rocky Mountains of Colorado, it took me a long time to decompress, finally realizing my previous pace was probably a fast track to an early heart attack.

We need to slow down, quiet our minds, get sufficient sleep, smile more often, and read some good books, even perhaps some good poetry, realizing there is more to life than speed.

PRACTICAL APPLICATIONS

1. Are you caught in the frenetic pace?
2. How can you build some quiet, calm moments into your day: chatting with an old friend, playing with children, or going for a walk in nature?
3. Block some time on your planner now just for slowing down.

Good leaders know they need to slow their pace at times.

THE GAMBLER

DON SCHLITZ

On a warm summer's eve
On a train bound for nowhere
I met up with the gambler
We were both too tired to sleep
So we took turns a-starin'
Out the window at the darkness
The boredom overtook us, he began to speak

He said, "Son, I've made a life
Out of readin' people's faces
Knowin' what the cards were
By the way they held their eyes
So if you don't mind me sayin'
I can see you're out of aces
For a taste of your whiskey
I'll give you some advice"
...
He said, "If you're gonna play the game, boy
You gotta learn to play it right

You've got to know when to hold 'em
Know when to fold 'em
Know when to walk away
Know when to run
You never count your money
When you're sittin' at the table
There'll be time enough for countin'
When the dealin's done

Every gambler knows
That the secret to survivin'
Is knowin' what to throw away
And knowin' what to keep
'Cause every hand's a winner
And every hand's a loser
And the best that you can hope for
Is to die in your sleep."

THEME

PLAYING THE HANDS YOU'RE DEALT

Don Schlitz (1952–) wrote the lyrics of "The Gambler" in 1978. Grammy award-winner and Country Music Hall of Fame singer, Kenny Rogers (1938–), recorded the song, and it became a #1 hit.

The lyrics of "The Gambler" have a leadership message that I like (perhaps because I also enjoy a good poker game?). In poker, every hand is a potential winner and a potential loser. It's how you read your adversaries and then how you play the cards you're dealt: knowing when to hold 'em, bluff, check, raise lightly, go "all in," and when, especially, to fold 'em. Too many poor poker players overplay marginal hands. They lose.

Life deals us all different hands. Actor Christopher Reeve, for example, was a talented, all-around athlete, who had a promising career in Hollywood, especially after his starring role in *Superman*. Then he was thrown from a horse in 1995 and paralyzed. He became an outspoken advocate for stem cell research and treatments for spinal cord injuries. He went on to star in television shows and raise money for those injured as he was. He used his Hollywood celebrity in ways he had never imagined. Reeve is quoted as saying,

You play the hand you're dealt.
I think the game's worthwhile.

Reeve played the bad cards life had dealt him and found in them some inspiring winners. Even after his tragic accident, he made sure his life was still "worthwhile."

How we play the hands life deals us is up to each of us. We can become a bitter victim, withdraw, and become a recluse, or reach out to influence others, to lead, in ways that have extraordinary impact.

PRACTICAL APPLICATIONS

1. What kind of hands has life dealt you?
2. Are you holding good cards, or weak ones?
3. How might you play your weak hands to turn them into winners?

Leading well means making winners from whatever hands you're dealt.

CASEY AT THE BAT

ERNEST LAWRENCE THAYER

The outlook wasn't brilliant for the Mudville nine that day:
The score stood four to two, with but one inning more to play
...

A straggling few got up to go in deep despair. The rest
Clung to the hope which springs eternal in the human breast;
They thought, "If only Casey could but get a whack at that-
We'd put up even money now, with Casey at the bat
...

But Flynn let drive a single, to the wonderment of all,
And Blake, the much despisèd, tore the cover off the ball
...

There was ease in Casey's manner as he stepped into his place;
There was pride in Casey's bearing and a smile lit Casey's face.
And when, responding to the cheers, he lightly doffed his hat,
No stranger in the crowd could doubt 'twas Casey at the bat
....

And now the leather-covered sphere came hurtling through the air,
And Casey stood a-watching it in haughty grandeur there.
Close by the sturdy batsman the ball unheeded sped-
"That ain't my style," said Casey. "Strike one!" the umpire said
...

With a smile of Christian charity great Casey's visage shone;
He stilled the rising tumult; he bade the game go on;
He signaled to the pitcher, and once more the dun [dull gray] sphere flew;
But Casey still ignored it and the umpire said, "Strike two!"
...

The sneer is gone from Casey's lip, his teeth are clenched in hate,
He pounds with cruel violence his bat upon the plate;
And now the pitcher holds the ball, and now he lets it go,
And now the air is shattered by the force of Casey's blow.

Oh, somewhere in this favoured land the sun is shining bright,
The band is playing somewhere, and somewhere hearts are light;
And somewhere men are laughing, and somewhere children shout,
But there is no joy in Mudville-mighty Casey has struck out.

THEME

CONQUERING EGO

"Casey at the Bat" was written in 1888 by American writer Ernest Thayer (1863–1940).[7] The *Baseball Almanac* called it "the nation's best-known piece of comic verse..."[8] I encourage you to read the whole poem. It's fun.

One danger of leadership is that, ironically, the more successful leaders are, the more they are vulnerable to hubris, which often results in failure. One would sense the opposite: the more successful leaders are, the more useful and valuable experience they have, allowing them to build on their successes. But human nature often intervenes in the form of the ego.

Many people want to be viewed positively by their leader, so they tend to be effusive in their praise, lauding the leader for his or her success. They filter out bad information that might make them, or the leader, look bad. Some people become sycophants. Soon, the leader becomes isolated and insulated. Leaders start to breathe their own vapor, believing their own press releases, or as they say in Texas, "All hat; no cattle." Or, as they say in Silicon Valley, "All slides; no product."

Casey is an icon in Mudville. The fans know they can win if only Casey can get to bat. He knows it too. He's been seduced by his own fame and arrogantly lets the first two pitches fly by unheeded, confident he can crush the next pitch out of the park. Imagine the shocked fans and the embarrassed Casey when he whiffs. Mouths must have dropped in stunned silence. "Mighty Casey has struck out."

How can a leader avoid this haughty ego trap?

- Be aware that you become more vulnerable to fail after a string of successes.
- Make it clear to your colleagues you want the unvarnished truth, not happy talk or whispers in your ear about how good you are.
- Never shoot the messenger who brings bad news. On the contrary, reward that messenger for truth-telling.
- Circulate often among all your stakeholders, soliciting their honest feedback.
- Have a trusted group of colleagues who will periodically give you constructive feedback, even being willing to tell you you've been acting like a jerk.

PRACTICAL APPLICATIONS

1. Make it clear to your team you want the truth.
2. Get out from behind your desk and circulate often to truly listen to people.
3. Enlist a group of colleagues who will level with each other and with you.
4. Remain humble.

Good leaders conquer their egos.

TEACHING YOU

JACKSON KIDDARD

Anything that annoys you is for teaching you patience.

Anyone who abandons you is for teaching you to stand up on your own two feet.

Anything that angers you is for teaching you forgiveness and compassion.

Anything that has power over you is for teaching you how to take your power back.

Anything you hate is for teaching you unconditional love.

Anything you fear is for teaching you courage to overcome your fear.

Anything you can't control is for teaching you how to let go and trust the Universe.

THEME

TEACHING YOU

Jackson Kiddard was an elusive author about whom little is known. He is believed to have died in 1901, and his work is now widely circulated on the internet. His short verses about "anything" or "anyone" are a treasure of practical wisdom.

We have much to learn if we can get out of our instinctual and often emotional reactions. As Nobel Prize winner Daniel Kahneman wrote in his insightful book *Thinking Fast and Slow,* we have two systems in our brains: System I and System II. System I is automatic, involuntary, and fast, with feelings emerging from our primitive instincts. System II is more controlled, effortful, and rational, working more slowly and rationally.

The System I brain sees round coils in a dark corner, and our heart spikes into our constricted throat as we sense a huge snake. Then the System II brain registers a coiled rope and our pulse, blood pressure, and adrenalin slowly begin to return to normal.

We need to be aware of our Systems I and II and manage between them accordingly:

- The construction stop on the freeway annoys us. Take a breath, wave, and smile at the person holding the "Slow" sign. Maybe you might even get a smile back?
- We humans fear abandonment, so we seek love and affection, often in all the wrong places.
- Leadership can be either fear-based (triggering System I) or love-based (triggering System II).
- Fears faced teach us courage.
- Control is an illusion. We can barely control ourselves, let alone others, so we learn to work on what we can influence and just let go of other things.

All challenges we face are potential gifts if we ask, "What is the lesson that I can learn from this adversity?" It takes self-control, discipline, presence of mind, patience, and practice to moderate the quick-snap reactions of System I, dampening the emotional knee jerks. However, these skills can be learned.

PRACTICAL APPLICATIONS

1. When you encounter an emotional reaction today, practice your self-control.
2. Tomorrow, practice it again.
3. Repeat until this practice becomes a habit.

Good leaders learn to balance between their emotional and logical minds.

DESIDERATA

MAX EHRMANN

Go placidly amid the noise and haste, and remember what peace there may be in silence.

As far as possible, without surrender, be on good terms with all persons. Speak your truth quietly and clearly; and listen to others, even to the dull and the ignorant, they too have their story. Avoid loud and aggressive persons, they are vexations to the spirit.

If you compare yourself with others, you may become vain and bitter; for always there will be greater and lesser persons than yourself. Enjoy your achievements as well as your plans. Keep interested in your own career, however humble; it is a real possession in the changing fortunes of time.

Exercise caution in your business affairs, for the world is full of trickery. But let this not blind you to what virtue there is; many persons strive for high ideals, and everywhere life is full of heroism. Be yourself. Especially, do not feign affection. Neither be cynical about love, for in the face of all aridity and disenchantment it is perennial as the grass.

Take kindly to the counsel of the years, gracefully surrendering the things of youth. Nurture strength of spirit to shield you in sudden misfortune. But do not distress yourself with imaginings. Many fears are born of fatigue and loneliness.

Beyond a wholesome discipline, be gentle with yourself. You are a child of the universe, no less than the trees and the stars; you have a right to be here. And whether or not it is clear to you, no doubt the universe is unfolding as it should.

Therefore, be at peace with God, whatever you conceive Him to be, and whatever your labors and aspirations, in the noisy confusion of life, keep peace in your soul.

With all its sham, drudgery and broken dreams, it is still a beautiful world.

Be cheerful. Strive to be happy.

THEME

BEING AT PEACE

Desiderata are those things necessary or highly desirable in life. "Desiderata" was written in 1927 by American author Max Ehrmann (1872–1945). A native of Terra Haute, Indiana, he had a common sense, down-to-earth message for all of us.

With today's 24/7 negative news cycle citing one outrage after another and reporting all the sham and trickery in the world, it's easy to become jaded and cynical about people. Too often, we chase the material trappings life offers: prestige, power, more toys, or the fantasies of escape now so prevalent. Too often, we stress about inconsequential things. Too often, we beat ourselves up with negative thoughts, demeaning and victimizing ourselves.

Ehrmann implores us to see the beauty in the world, to treasure silence, and to listen to the sounds of nature. He exhorts us to be gentle with ourselves as children of the universe, and to be at peace with God, whatever we conceive God to be. He recognizes that there are many heroes and heroines among us in everyday life: the teachers, firefighters, nurses, truck drivers, factory workers, mothers, grandparents, and more. Many of these people manifest the virtues and values we all inherently admire.

Before we can lead ourselves, or presume to lead others, in the noise and haste of this frantic life we create for ourselves, we must first be at peace with our souls. Then the true joy in this beautiful world can be rediscovered.

PRACTICAL APPLICATIONS

1. Are you gentle with yourself, or hypercritically comparing yourself with others?
2. Do you find times for quiet reflection?
3. Do you see more beauty in life, or is your view of people jaded and cynical?
4. Are you at peace with your soul?

Good leaders have an inner peace and presence that radiates out, resonating with people and drawing them close.

STEEL AND VELVET

CARL SANDBURG

Not often in the story of mankind does a man arrive on earth who is both steel and velvet, who is as hard as rock and soft as drifting fog, who holds in his heart and mind the paradox of terrible storm and peace unspeakable and perfect.

...

Infinitely tender was his word from a White House balcony to a crowd on the White House lawn,-"I have not willingly planted a thorn in any man's bosom, or a military governor,-I shall do nothing through malice; what I deal with is too vast for malice."

THEME

FLEXING BETWEEN STEEL AND VELVET

The words about steel and velvet are excerpts from a speech Carl Sandburg (1878–1967) delivered before a Joint Session of Congress in 1959 on Abraham Lincoln's 150th birthday. Sandberg was an immensely talented American writer and poet who won three Pulitzer Prizes, one for his biography of Lincoln. Upon Sandberg's death, U. S. President Lyndon Johnson said,

Carl Sandburg was more than the voice of America,
more than the poet of its strength and genius. He was America.[9]

Sandburg considered Abraham Lincoln to be an extraordinary leader. Lincoln was able to flex between what Sandburg called steel and velvet. (Gregg and I describe steel and velvet in detail in *Triple Crown Leadership* as the hard and soft edges of leadership.[10]) Lincoln was steel because he made the tough decisions that leadership sometimes demands. He imposed martial law, instituted the first military conscription, suspended habeas corpus, and freed the slaves in the Confederate States through the Emancipation Proclamation, which he personally drafted.

But Lincoln also led with a softer, velvet touch. He persuasively influenced people during personal visits to their offices or the battlefields. He listened deeply and engaged in mischievous storytelling, loving good jokes. He often sought input from others, even his rivals, asking for guidance, and learning from their counsel.

Over the years, I slowly learned that good leaders know when to flex between the hard and soft edges of leadership. I couldn't stay stuck in my personality profile, which is primarily steel. Because I tend to be talkative and creative with ideas, often too intense and impatient, I had to learn to dial it down, letting others talk and lead at times. But there were times when I had to mandate certain principles: "We will achieve our results ethically. No exceptions."

At times, a good leader must be steel: exercising authority, title, and power. Much more often, that same leader must be velvet: listening, asking questions, and letting others lead. The key is to flex your leadership style according to the people involved and the urgency of the situation.

PRACTICAL APPLICATIONS

1. Are you more steel or velvet?
2. Do you flex your style, or are you stuck in one mode?
3. Who can give you feedback on your leadership flexibility?

Leading well means flexing between the hard and soft edges of leadership.

TWO WOLVES

AUTHOR UNKNOWN

One evening, an old Cherokee Indian told his grandson about a battle that goes on inside people. He said, "My son, the battle is between two wolves inside us all. One is Evil. It is anger, envy, jealousy, sorrow, regret, greed, arrogance, self-pity, guilt, resentment, inferiority, lies, false pride, superiority, and ego. The other is Good. It is joy, peace, love, hope, serenity, humility, kindness, benevolence, empathy, generosity, truth, compassion and faith." The grandson thought about it for a minute and then asked his grandfather: "Which wolf wins?"

The grandfather replied, "The one you feed."

THEME

HAVING A POSITIVE MINDSET

This simple parable, whose Native American author has been lost to time, conveys a powerful message to me. So much of life, success, and leadership are the products of one's mind.

Which set of thoughts do we choose to feed: cynicism, impatience, wallowing, power, vengeance, deceit, control, fear, victimhood, jealousy, and the like? The wise Cherokee grandfather called those types of thoughts "evil."

Or do we choose to feed: community, respect, trust, civility, integrity, honor, courage, love, and the like? The Cherokee grandfather called those types of thoughts the "good."

There is an ongoing battle inside our minds between good and evil, between what's right and what's expedient, between what our conscience can live with and what we can get away with.

Early in life I often carried a chip on my shoulder. I was impatient, harboring negative thoughts about people, and too quick to anger. I considered myself a loner at work. This mindset that I unconsciously fed with my thoughts didn't work well. I learned to change my mindset. It took time and practice, lots of practice, but now, I'm a bit wiser and better at managing my thoughts.

Leaders face reality. They don't sugarcoat the challenges of our world. But leaders don't run around with a negative cloud over their heads. They see the good that's possible and work diligently to make it the reality.

In the fifth century BCE, the Buddha said it too:

All that we are is the result of what we have thought.
The mind is everything. What we think, we become.

PRACTICAL APPLICATIONS

1. What types of thoughts feed your mind?

    a. Is your mindset negative, often seeing all that's wrong, whining and complaining about the scarcity, the inequality, and the unfairness?

    b. Or, is your mindset positive, often seeing what's good, encouraging others, smiling at the abundance that can be created, and taking on the travails of the day with optimism that they can be overcome?

2. Make a list today of the things you could do to change your mindset to focus on the "good."

Good leadership begins with the thoughts you choose to feed.

TO BE OR NOT TO BE

WILLIAM SHAKESPEARE

To be, or not to be, that is the question:
Whether 'tis Nobler in the mind to suffer
The Slings and Arrows of outrageous Fortune,
Or to take Arms against a Sea of troubles,
And by opposing end them: to die, to sleep
No more; and by a sleep, to say we end
The Heartache, and the thousand Natural shocks
That Flesh is heir to? 'Tis a consummation
Devoutly to be wished. To die, to sleep,
To sleep, perchance to Dream; aye, there's the rub,
For in that sleep of death, what dreams may come,
When we have shuffled off this mortal coil,
Must give us pause. There's the respect
That makes Calamity [disaster] of so long life:
For who would bear the Whips and Scorns of time,
The Oppressor's wrong, the proud man's Contumely [contempt],
The pangs of despised Love, the Law's delay,
The insolence of Office, and the Spurns
That patient merit of the unworthy takes,
When he himself might his Quietus [death] make
With a bare Bodkin [tool]? Who would Fardels [burdens] bear,
To grunt and sweat under a weary life,
But that the dread of something after death,
The undiscovered Country, from whose bourn [boundary]
No Traveler returns, Puzzles the will,
And makes us rather bear those ills we have,
Than fly to others that we know not of.
Thus Conscience does make Cowards of us all,
And thus the Native hue of Resolution
Is sicklied o'er, with the pale cast of Thought,
And enterprises of great pitch [essence] and moment,
With this regard their Currents turn awry [away],
And lose the name of Action.

THEME

BEING DECISIVE

William Shakespeare (1564–1616), the "Bard of Avon," was an English poet, playwright, and actor, widely regarded as the greatest writer in the English language. He wrote 38 plays and 154 sonnets. His plays have been translated into every major language and are performed more often than those of any other playwright.[11]

"To be or not to be" is from a soliloquy in Shakespeare's play *Hamlet.* Here, the Prince of Denmark considers death and suicide given the pains and unfairness of his life ("the slings and arrows of outrageous Fortune"). His uncle, Claudius, has murdered the former king, Hamlet's father, and become Hamlet's stepfather by hurriedly marrying Hamlet's mother. Hamlet hesitates to avenge his father's murder and vacillates on taking his own life, thinking deeply: "to be or not to be"? Is death possibly worse than the woeful life of his tortured soul? Hamlet fears what might lie beyond death, and moans that the "pale cast of thought" overcomes resolute action. Hamlet thinks too much, and in so doing he fails to act.

The plot of *Hamlet* is rich with many complex themes involving power, murder, revenge, palace intrigue, and numerous sub-plots. But I interpret *Hamlet's* "to be or not to be" soliloquy as dealing with indecision. Too often, we think too much, pondering this alternative or that alternative, turning away from actions of great importance. We form a committee to discuss the issue. We ask for more information before deciding. Then we want more information. We procrastinate because making tough decisions is difficult.

One of the lessons I learned in corporate turnarounds is that quick decisions are sometimes necessary. Not always; sometimes contemplation and reflection are helpful, requiring deep consideration. But in a crisis when the pressure is on, one must act decisively. One may not be sure a course of action is 100 percent right, but one needs to decide and act, making the inevitable midcourse corrections later.

PRACTICAL APPLICATIONS

1. Is there an important decision you have been avoiding?
2. Why not make a decision today and begin to implement it?

When the pressure is on, good leaders are decisive.

UNTIL ONE IS COMMITTED

WILLIAM HUTCHINSON MURRAY

Until one is committed, there is hesitancy, the chance to draw back, always ineffectiveness.

Concerning all acts of initiative (and creation), there is one elementary truth, the ignorance of which kills countless ideas and splendid plans: that the moment one definitely commits oneself, then Providence moves too. All sorts of things occur to help one that would never otherwise have occurred. A whole stream of events issues from the decision, raising in one's favour all manner of unforeseen incidents and meetings and material assistance, which no man could have dreamt would have come his way. I learned a deep respect for one of Goethe's couplets: "Whatever you can do or dream you can, begin it. Boldness has genius, power and magic in it."

THEME

MAKING BOLD COMMITMENTS

This passage is generally attributed to German author, Johann Wolfgang von Goethe (1749–1832). The actual source is writer William Hutchinson Murray (1913–1996), a Scottish mountaineer, in his book *The Scottish Himalayan Expedition* (1951). Murray acknowledges Goethe's couplet as his inspiration at the close.

These inspiring lines contain an important message about commitment. Living a good life and being a good leader are lifelong challenges. We will encounter all forms of adversity. Too many of us fail to make bold commitments. We hold back, hesitate, ponder the effort required, and, as a result, live our lives as pale shadows of what we might have become. We are indecisive, as Hamlet's "To be or not to be" soliloquy illustrates. But even beyond indecision and vacillation, we are not bold enough in our decisions; we are too mild-mannered in our actions.

My own experience echoes Murray's words about commitment. In challenging corporate turnarounds, I was often astonished at the accomplishments a small band of committed people could achieve. Once we commit, the laws of gravity holding us down are released. Somehow, Providence moves. Colleagues arrive to assist. Ideas and creations we were never aware of before suddenly pop into our attention. Locked doors open. New windows appear through which we can climb into new venues.

Inevitably, we have to make adjustments and alterations along the way. Plans will have to be revised. But the mighty quest is joined because bold commitment, indeed, has "genius, power, and magic in it," inspiring others to join the worthy cause.

PRACTICAL APPLICATIONS

1. Can you recall a time you made a bold commitment and suddenly new ideas and opportunities emerged, almost as if by "magic"?

2. Why not overcome any hesitancy and make a new, bold commitment today, beginning it right *now*?

Leading well requires making bold commitments.

INVICTUS

WILLIAM ERNEST HENLEY

Out of the night that covers me,
Black as the pit from pole to pole,
I thank whatever gods may be
For my unconquerable soul.

In the fell clutch of circumstance
I have not winced nor cried aloud.
Under the bludgeonings of chance
My head is bloody, but unbowed.

Beyond this place of wrath and tears
Looms but the horror of the shade,
And yet the menace of the years
Finds, and shall find, me unafraid.

It matters not how strait [narrow, difficult] the gate,
How charged with punishments the scroll,
I am the master of my fate:
I am the captain of my soul.

THEME

MASTERING YOUR FATE

William Ernest Henley (1849–1903) was a poet, critic, and editor in the late-Victorian era in England. His most famous poem, "Invictus," was written in 1875.

Henley describes the stark realities of life that we all experience: the black night, the bloody bludgeoning, the wrath and tears, and then the shady darkness of death. But the poet remains undaunted: not wincing, head unbowed, unafraid, the captain of his unconquerable soul, and the master of his fate.

How can Henley's poet be so strong and fearless? Note he refers to the gods, whoever they may be, so he believes in some higher power or powers. And one noun is used twice: "soul." He refers to that soul as "unconquerable." Think about that word: "unconquerable." Nothing, *nothing*, in this physical world can defeat his soul if he fearlessly faces the challenges life brings.

But even more, the horror of the shade of death leaves him unafraid, even though his gate into Heaven may be narrow and difficult to enter because of the punishments he has accumulated on the scroll of his life.

The poet is certain that if he refuses to be a victim of fate, passively accepting its blows, if he works tirelessly for what is right, if he masters fate by the tough choices he makes, then his unconquerable, immortal soul is eternally safe.

How many of us have this certainty? How many of us fall victim to whining, wallowing, and wailing about what fate has wrought upon us? Leaders don't moan and offer excuses. They tirelessly, fearlessly remain undaunted.

Invictus is Latin for "unconquered."

PRACTICAL APPLICATIONS

1. Are you a muttering moaner?
2. What might you do today to show your fearless resolve to master your fate?
3. Think of three positive actions you can start doing today that will help you conquer your fears.

Good leadership involves captaining your own ship to master your fate.

I AM ONLY ONE

EDWARD EVERETT HALE

I am only one, but still I am one. I cannot do everything, but still I can do something. And because I cannot do everything, I will not refuse to do the something that I can do.

THEME

DOING SOMETHING

Edward Everett Hale (1822–1909) was an American author, historian, and Unitarian minister. Hale was the grandnephew of Revolutionary War hero Nathan Hale, who was captured on an intelligence-gathering mission and hanged by the British as a spy. Nathan Hale's famous final words were:

I only regret that I have but one life to give for my country.

Edward Everett Hale's poem extols the contribution all of us can make, even though the challenge seems vast. A corporate board once dismissed me from a very challenging CEO assignment due to a lagging stock price. I had spent several years executing a brutal turnaround, our extraordinary leadership team had virtually reinvented the company, and great progress was being made as evidenced by a huge swing in cash flow from negative to positive. But the stock price had still not recovered, a key indicator for Wall Street and the board. When my dismissal came, I was distraught and depressed. I felt like a failure.

But what we accomplished over my several years at the company hit me most dramatically when I stepped out onto a balcony in the atrium of our headquarters to give my final farewell remarks. The huge crowd of employees gathered began to clap, and they just wouldn't stop. On and on, they continued clapping, clapping, clapping. Their expression of appreciation brought tears to my eyes. I realized they knew what we had done together, and my heart, once again, went out to them.

Like Nathan Hale, I may not have accomplished all I had hoped to do, but I had given the best of my corporate-life skills to that firm and met my corporate death there in the process. I had made great progress on my life's purpose: to leave that company and its people, my little world at the time, in a better place.

PRACTICAL APPLICATIONS

1. What is something that you can do towards a worthy cause?

2. Can you identify at least three other allies who might join you in this cause?

3. Can you meet with those allies today and start a conversation about what you can do together?

4. Even if you have no allies to join you at first, is it possible that, by making your commitment, others will join you later?

Leading well means doing whatever you can do, even if the cause seems daunting.

IF I CAN STOP ONE HEART FROM BREAKING

EMILY DICKINSON

If I can stop one heart from breaking

I shall not live in vain

If I can ease one Life the Aching

Or cool one Pain

Or help one fainting Robin

Unto his Nest again,

I shall not live in Vain.

THEME

HELPING JUST ONE

Emily Dickinson (1830–1886) was an American poet who was considered to be an eccentric recluse by many of her neighbors in Amherst, Massachusetts. Curiously, she frequently dressed all in white and sometimes spoke to visitors from the other side of a door. Deeply creative people can be a little quirky, so we need to cut them some slack. Most of Dickinson's 1800 poems were published posthumously.[12]

"If I Can Stop One Heart from Breaking" appeals to me because it's about life being worthwhile if one is helping or serving just one other person. My colleague and friend Bob Whipple says,

When we look back at our lives, the thing we remember most is not the pile of clutter we have collected, or the awards we have won, it is who we have helped along the way.

Leadership doesn't have to be about commanding armies, becoming a CEO, or saving the world. My talented sister, Ann, became a nurse. With her husband, Jim, and other family members, she founded and successfully ran a wonderful home health care agency in Texas that still serves many people, especially infants who were in serious danger when they were released from the hospital. Ann never focused on commanding legions or building a huge company, but on helping one person at a time.

My sister is a caring, loving person. She led, and continues to lead, in extraordinary ways, impacting her family, neighbors, the community, and many thankful patients, making a huge difference in their lives one at a time. She tells me,

Leadership can be that one takes the lead when they see someone, or an animal, that has a need that one can fulfill, and they step up to the plate and do it.
I did love seeing people get better, or learning to cope with their health problems better, because of what my staff or I did.
I guess I am still driven by trying to ease someone's life challenges.

Ann is true to the spirit of Emily Dickinson's poem and a leader I admire.

Regardless of your circumstances in life, regardless of the burdens you carry, you can help heal a broken heart, help relieve someone's pain, or just help a robin back into her nest.

PRACTICAL APPLICATIONS

1. Who are some people you can help today?

2. What might you do today to bring a ray of sunshine into their lives?

3. Why not pick up the phone, or, even better, go see that person right now?

Helping even just one other person is good leadership.

TO RISK

AUTHOR UNKNOWN

To laugh ... is to risk appearing the fool.

To cry ... is to risk appearing sentimental.

To reach out ... is to risk involvement.

To expose your feelings ... is to risk exposing your true self.

To place your ideas and dreams before a crowd ... is to risk rejection.

To love ... is to risk not being loved in return.

To live ... is to risk dying.

To hope ... is to risk despair.

To try ... is to risk failure.

But risks must be taken, because the greatest hazard in life is to risk nothing.

Those who risk nothing, do nothing, and have nothing.

They may avoid suffering and sorrow,

but they cannot learn, feel, change, grow, or love.

Chained by their certitude, they are slaves;

they have forfeited their freedom.

Only one who risks is truly free...

THEME

TAKING RISKS

Authorship of "To Risk" is often attributed to author Leo Buscaglia, but it has also been credited to Ralph Waldo Emerson, or Janet Rand, which may be a pseudonym for Louise L. Wilson. The true author may actually be William Arthur Ward (1921–1994), one of America's most quoted writers of inspirational verse, and may have originally been titled "The Dilemma."[13] I can't verify who the true author is of the poem "To Risk."

Life and leadership all involve risk and overcoming our natural and normal fears. Leadership is a choice. One *decides* to lead something. That's a risk. Some will carp about your presumptuousness. Some will complain about your choices. Some will second-guess how you went about leading. That's all normal. Critics complain. Leaders lead.

As John Paul Jones, the American Revolutionary War naval hero, said,

> *It seems to be a law of nature, inflexible, and inexorable,*
> *that those who will not risk cannot win.*

In my youth, and even through my early career, I had a deep, gut-level fear of public speaking. Not just the normal fear of public speaking, but intense, nausea-inducing, throat-constricting fear because I stuttered. Sometimes, when I knew my turn to speak was near, I'd excuse myself, find a faraway bathroom, lock the door, and let out a primal scream to release the tension.

Eventually, I enrolled in public speaking courses where I practiced, practiced and practiced, over and over again, driving down the fear, until I finally could speak persuasively in public. I took the risk of embarrassment, which was huge to me at the time, and conquered it.

You may not choose to lead all the time. That's fine. But it's highly likely that at some time you will have a leadership choice to make: "Should I speak up now and risk looking foolish, being embarrassed, or incurring someone's wrath?" A better question to ask yourself will be: "Can I live with my conscience if I don't speak up and lead?"

Risk exists for all of us. But as our unknown poet says, those who don't risk can't truly learn to feel, grow, and love.

PRACTICAL APPLICATIONS

1. What's a topic that you feel you should speak up about but haven't?
2. What has been holding you back?
3. Can you think of ways to overcome what's been holding you back?
4. Can you live with a clean conscience if you don't speak up and lead?

Good leadership involves overcoming our natural fears and taking risks.

DON'T QUIT

EDGAR GUEST

When Things go wrong, as they sometimes will,
When the road you're trudging seems all uphill,
When the funds are low and debts are high,
And you want to Smile but have to sigh.
When care is pressing you down a bit,
Rest, if you must, but don't you quit.

Life is queer with its twists and turns,
As everyone of us sometimes learns,
And many a failure turns about,
When he might have won if he'd stuck it out,
Don't give up though the pace seems slow,
You might succeed with another blow.

Often the struggler has given up,
When he might have captured the victor's cup.
And he learned too late, when the night slipped down,
How close he was to the golden crown,

Success is failure turned inside out,
The silver tint of clouds of doubt,
And you never can tell how close you are,
It may be near when it seems afar,
So stick to the fight when you're hardest hit,
It's when things seem worst that you mustn't quit.

THEME

PERSEVERING

Edgar Guest (1881–1959) was an English-born American poet, who became popular in the United States as the "people's poet." He wrote over 11,000 poems, many of which appeared in his syndicated newspaper columns.[14]

The theme of persevering in "Don't Quit" implores us to stay the course and "carry on," as the British did so well in World War II. Recall Winston Churchill's words,

If you're going through hell, keep going.

I am reminded of the difficult turnaround work I often undertook during my career. My quest was to find a better way to lead, and I didn't want to search for it in the halls of academia, nor through consulting on changes someone else would implement. I wanted to experience it, taste it, and feel it through the challenges of really leading something. My choice of what to lead was not stable, successful firms with bright futures, but companies facing huge challenges: lawsuits, ethical malfeasance, technology shifts, daunting quality defects, disaffected employees and customers, and more. If I could learn to lead successfully in those circumstances, then many of the lessons would surely apply in easier terrains.

But I learned how daunting turnaround leadership could be. In the midst of these formidable challenges, we knew that things would definitely get worse before they got better. We referenced Murphy's Law: "Anything that can go wrong will go wrong." It's a pessimistic outlook, but we joked that Murphy was an optimist. We thought of the turnaround as organ donations: each of us giving a lung, a kidney, our spleens, and more to save the corpus. Sometimes humor is the best way to deal with adversity.

Still, we soldiered on, discovering that what humans had led asunder, they could resurrect, oftentimes even better than it was before. On the steep uphill roads that seemed to go on forever, we just didn't quit.

PRACTICAL APPLICATIONS

1. How impossible does the road you have chosen seem to be?
2. Can you hang in there just one more day at a time, refusing to quit?
3. Then just one more day?

Good leaders persevere.

PSALM 23

HEBREW BIBLE/OLD TESTAMENT

The Lord is my shepherd

I shall not want.

He maketh me to lie down in green pastures

He leadeth me beside the still waters.

He restoreth my soul

He leadeth me in the paths of righteousness for his name's sake.

Yea, though I walk through the valley of the shadow of death,

I will fear no evil

For thou art with me

Thy rod and thy staff they comfort me.

Thou preparest a table before me in the presence of mine enemies

Thou anointest my head with oil

My cup runneth over.

Surely goodness and mercy shall follow me all the days of my life

And I will dwell in the house of the Lord forever.

THEME

TRUSTING A HIGHER POWER

"Psalm 23" is from the Book of Psalms in the Old Testament and the Hebrew Bible. This translation is from the King James Bible. Some scholars attribute it to King David (1040–970 BCE). David was the second king of Israel, an ancestor of Jesus, a courageous warrior and a poet credited with composing much of the Book of Psalms.[15] In this beautiful psalm, God is portrayed as a good shepherd, as Jesus is portrayed as a shepherd in the New Testament's Gospel of John.

I take comfort from these verses knowing that, even in the depths of despair, I can turn for comfort and fortitude to a higher power. You might call the higher power God, Lord, Jesus, Allah, Jehovah, or another name. You might feel the higher power is in nature, or in the community of souls through which we are all connected. You might feel that a higher power is found in love. I sense they are all the same and are a mystery that is beyond my understanding. I have learned to live with and accept that mystery.

No matter what your spiritual beliefs may be, many people, like me, find solace in believing they do not walk alone. We are connected to something stronger, higher, better, and eternal, something beyond our mortal comprehension.

Even in our darkest moments, even in the presence of overwhelming adversity, we can trust our higher power understands, radiates love, and figuratively walks beside us, providing us the strength to carry on and do what's right.

Leaders often face great adversity. Few of the great leaders of history were atheists. Most exemplary leaders in history found comfort and strength in their belief and trust in a higher power.

PRACTICAL APPLICATIONS

1. Do you believe in a higher power, something beyond your own self, beyond your own ego?
2. Have there been times you have turned to that higher power for comfort or courage?
3. Take some time today to turn to your higher power, whatever you believe that may be, expressing your thanks, confirming your belief, and reaffirming your commitment.
4. Then just listen for the message you'll receive.

Leading well often involves trusting a higher power.

SEA FEVER

JOHN MASEFIELD

I must go down to the seas again, to the lonely sea and the sky,
And all I ask is a tall ship and a star to steer her by;
And the wheel's kick and the wind's song and the white sail's shaking,
And a grey mist on the sea's face, and a grey dawn breaking.

I must go down to the seas again, for the call of the running tide
Is a wild call and a clear call that may not be denied;
And all I ask is a windy day with the white clouds flying,
And the flung spray and the blown spume, and the sea-gulls crying.

I must go down to the seas again, to the vagrant gypsy life,
To the gull's way and the whale's way where the wind's like a whetted knife;
And all I ask is a merry yarn from a laughing fellow-rover,
And quiet sleep and a sweet dream when the long trick's over.

THEME

FINDING SANCTUARY

John Masefield (1878–1967) was an English poet and the Poet Laureate of the United Kingdom from 1930 to 1967, forty-seven years, an extraordinary accomplishment. His 1902 poem "Sea Fever" describes a longing the poet has for the sea. The writer sees, hears, and feels the sea with all of his senses.

We all have a deep longing for some place of refuge or sanctuary where we can retreat from the hectic world we create for ourselves. That place might be the ocean, a deep forest, majestic mountains, or a sandy beach. It might be a quiet cabin by a lake, or possibly meditation or prayer in a church, synagogue, temple, or mosque. No matter where our refuge may be, each of us must at times retreat to that place of sanctuary and replenishment to be renewed and refreshed.

Too often during my career, I took little or no vacation and worked too many hours. Once I boarded an airplane with two packed-full briefcases of reading material to plough through. Once seated, I focused intensely on my work, discarding pages around my feet. The flight attendant commented, "I have never seen anyone work so intently on a flight." Perhaps she meant it as a compliment, but I don't think so. For too long, I missed the boat on sanctuary.

My father worked in a noisy, dirty factory most of his life to support our family. He hated it. He often took me fishing at Chicago's Lake Front, or on Eagle Lake in Wisconsin, and once up to Canada. I loved it. But after he died, I lost my bearings and forgot or disregarded the need for places of refuge. Now, much older, I've found my sanctuary in the Rocky Mountains. I only wish I'd found it sooner. But it's never too late for you to find your sanctuary.

PRACTICAL APPLICATIONS

1. What place of sanctuary does your heart long for?

2. How long has it been since you've been there?

3. Put some times in your planner today to go back to your sanctuary and reflect on what you are doing with your life

Leading well means refreshing in places of sanctuary.

IN THE DEEPS ARE THE VIOLENCE

ANNIE DILLARD

In the deeps are the violence and terror of which psychology has warned us. But if you ride these monsters deeper down, if you drop with them farther over the world's rim, you find what our sciences cannot locate or name, the substrate, the ocean or matrix or ether which buoys the rest, which gives goodness its power for good, and evil its power for evil, the unified field: our complex and inexplicable caring for each other, and for our life together here. This is given. It is not learned.

THEME

GOING DEEPER

Annie Dillard (1945–) is a Pulitzer Prize winning American author. The excerpt quoted here is from her 1985 book, *Teaching a Stone to Talk: Expeditions and Encounters*.

The theme of this excerpt is about going deeper, beyond the world we frantically run around in, below the id and ego that Freud and Jung analyzed, and somewhere over our tangible world's rim to a place beyond the reach of science. There, Dillard writes, we find what she calls the "unified field," the "ether" that is connecting us all.

I find Dillard's words both moving and intriguing. I have no idea what the unified field is, but I believe and trust that it's there, a rainbow of something beyond energy, cascading out from a higher power to every far corner of the universes that ever were, are now, or will be. It is the spiritual connection linking us all to the eternal and pervading everything.

Our rational minds may deny this ethereal dimension. We can't see it or confirm it, but that doesn't mean it's not there. I've sensed it in prayer and meditation. I've listened to it when I asked my inner voice for counsel. I've felt it in love for my soul mate, June, once I pushed my ego out of the way. I felt it in the love for my family, close and extended. I've felt it in the unbridled joy I experienced with colleagues as we accomplished what some thought impossible. I've learned it in the kindness, patience, and love of friends and in the lessons of extraordinary leaders I had the honor and privilege to meet and learn from.

The skeptics and logicians will sneer. I don't care. I've felt it, spoken with it, asked it for guidance, and thanked it often for the blessings and challenges I have been given. Call it what you will: the higher power, the unified field, the consciousness that transcends all, or just the ether. It's there, waiting for us, calling to us. Our responsibility is to go deeper, connecting with it and with each other.

PRACTICAL APPLICATIONS:

1. Do you believe in a higher power that connects us all?
2. Do you sense this dimension calls us to connect with each other?
3. What can you do today in your world to truly connect with others?

Good leaders connect with others.

WORK AND THE SOUL

DAVID WHYTE

... [the] soul evades the cage of definition. It is the indefinable essence of a person's spirit and being. It can never be touched and yet the merest hint of its absence causes immediate distress. In a work situation, its lack can be sensed intuitively, though a person may, at the same moment, be powerless to know what has caused the loss. It may be the ... inner intuitions of a path not taken.

...

Work has to do with cornering and controlling conscious life. It attempts concrete goals. It loves the linear and the defined. But the soul finds its existence through a loss of control to those powers greater than human experience.

Work helps us to feel safe. The soul is safe already. Safe in its own experience of the world. Work is bounded by time. The soul of a person lies outside of time and belongs to the unknown, it is the sacred otherness of existence. Work belongs to the personality, but the soul is owned by no one, not even by the personality formed around it. The personality will, we are continually amazed, kiss any required part of the anatomy to rise in the world; the soul refuses to kiss anything but life itself, and then, as Blake says, only as it flies.

Work is slowly mastered. The soul life of a person is always larger and greater the more we come to know it. We go to work. But it is our soul we put into it. Work is a series of events. The soul, as James Hillman says, turns those workaday events into experience.

...

The core of difficulty at the heart of modern work life is its abstraction from many of the ancient cycles of life that allow the silence and time in which true appreciation and experience can take place. The hurried child becomes the pressured student, and finally the harassed manager.

THEME

BRINGING YOUR SOUL TO WORK

David Whyte (1955–) grew up in Yorkshire, England, and now resides in the Pacific Northwest of the United States. He is an accomplished poet who brings his insights into human nature and the soul to his work as a consultant with many international companies. The passages above are taken from his wonderful book, *The Heart Aroused: Poetry and the Preservation of the Soul in Corporate America*.

Whyte encourages people to bring their souls to work. He defines soul as the "indefinable essence of a person's spirit and being [the] sacred otherness of existence." Without soul-based work, we are mere shadows of what we could be, hollowed-out minds and bodies driven by our fears and egos. By putting our souls into our work, the work becomes nobler, more of what our souls want us to be.

People have souls, or perhaps, as some scholars suggest, souls inhabit people. But can a corporation have a soul? The legal construct of a corporation limits its liability and gives it a license to operate, but of course corporations technically can't have souls.

If we take some poetic license, though, we might think of a corporation more broadly as a collection of people, past and present, who act together for certain purposes. These people impact other people: their stakeholders and the world. In that sense, we can see a collective corporate soul emerge as the cumulative result of past and present actions, as well as the future intentions, of the people in the corporation. Paraphrasing Whyte's words, we might see the corporate collective soul as that indefinable essence of the firm's spirit and being, its sacred otherness.

The essence of a high-performance team is greater and more impactful than the sum of the essences of the individual team members. They feed off each other, cover for each other's weaknesses, and achieve results far beyond the sum of their individual talents. A high-performance team has a collective soul, an essence, that exceeds their individual souls added together.

So, each of us needs to bring our body, mind, and soul to work in order to be fully present. Our souls need to be present to help create a healthy collective corporate soul because most of us fervently desire to be part of something far better than us, something with an indefinable essence that is good, noble, and inherently beautiful.

PRACTICAL APPLICATIONS

1. Are you bringing your soul to your work?
2. How might you better reflect in your work the spirit of who you truly are?
3. How might you enhance the collective soul of your organization?

Good leaders bring their souls into their work, contributing to the collective soul of their organizations.

PART II

LEADING OTHERS

Leadership and life are all about relationships.

So much of the leadership literature focuses on "the leader," what to do to become a better leader, how to dress and speak for success, how to manage people more effectively, or how to get people to do what you want them to do, ad nauseam.

Early in my career, I was a loner, well organized and a hard worker, but I just operated by myself. I worked with people, but I was not connected. We never got deep, or real, or built trust. It was all politely transactional: "You do this for me, and I'll do that for you."

Frankly, that loner approach didn't work. Over the years with patient coaching, I learned that none of us is smart enough, or can work enough hours, to get it all done. It takes relationships with people to succeed. Not transactional relationships, but transformational relationships in which we are open, build trust, and act ethically and respectfully, even in disagreement.

The power of those kinds of relationships, I discovered, is awesome. Groups of people in deep, trusting relationships have virtually no limits to what they can achieve.

Those relationships are not about "I'm the leader and follow me." In those relationships, leadership is dynamic, organic, like a living thing, ebbing and flowing among different people at different times depending on the situation, expertise, and passion of the people involved. Even in the hierarchy used by most organizations, leaders lead at times and at other times let others lead, especially those closest to the action and those on fire about a certain cause.

It takes courage to give up control and power, letting others lead, radically empowering them, and seeing your leadership as service that elevates others. It takes wisdom to base your interactions on love and trust rather than on fear and control. But the dividends are immense. I've seen and felt them. My colleagues and I soared together, and our lives changed.

Our focus should not be so much on an individual leader, but more on this dynamic, organic, relationship-based, caring activity that produces extraordinary results called "leadership." This refocus on the dynamic of leadership means we must shift our mindset and attitude about leading others. It's not about fear, control, power, being judgmental, and operating from the ego. Rather, good leadership cares for people, serving and empowering them. It starts with an open-minded understanding of where people currently are, building trust while holding them accountable for their commitments. Good leadership gently pushes people to courageously embrace needed change. In essence good leadership is rooted in love and compassion.

We can find deep wisdom about relationships, leading others, and the dynamic of leadership in poetry and prose.

HEART AND TRUST

PARKER PALMER

The best leaders work from a place of integrity in themselves, from their hearts. If they don't, they can't inspire trustful relationships. In the absence of trust, organizations fall apart

....

And what do people do in unsafe situations? They start hiding out. They start faking it. They start giving less than what they have to give. They start playing it close to the vest. An organization may "work" under these conditions but simply cannot function at anywhere near full effectiveness

....

I'm using the word heart as they did in ancient times, when it didn't merely mean the emotions, as it tends to mean today. It meant that center in the human self where everything comes together-where will and intellect and values and feeling and intuition and vision all converge. It meant the source of one's integrity. It takes courage to lead from the heart because you're putting your own identity and integrity into the public arena. You're standing for things you believe in.

THEME

LEADING WITH HEAD AND HEART

Parker Palmer (1939–) is a noted American educator and the best-selling author of *Let Your Life Speak* and *The Courage to Teach*. He made these observations about heart during an interview with L. J. Rittenhouse in 2001.[16]

Organizations today are suffering from a lack of engagement in many employees. Gallup surveys on employee engagement report that the average U.S. company in 2014 only had 31.5 percent of its employees engaged, while 51 percent were not engaged, and 17.5 percent were actively disengaged.[17] These results are not surprising given the Edelman surveys on trust in leaders. A 2013 Edelman survey showed that only 19 percent of those surveyed believe that business leaders will make ethical and moral decisions. For government leaders, it was only 14 percent.[18] Staggering results.

Too often, companies hire and promote people based on their "head" characteristics like intelligence, experience, skills, and technical proficiencies. Of course those qualities are important, but at the best organizations that Gregg and I researched for *Triple Crown Leadership*, we found that having these head characteristics was the minimum required to get hired or promoted.

More important are the "heart" qualities like integrity, character, emotional intelligence, and fit with the culture of the organization. Heart qualities build trust, engagement, and the soul of an organization. As Nelson Mandela once said,

A good head and a good heart are always a formidable combination.

An organization's soul resides in the collective beliefs, values, intentions, and actions of the people who work there. The collective soul of an organization progresses or regresses based on the heart-driven behaviors of its past and present people.

PRACTICAL APPLICATIONS

1. Are you hiring and promoting for both head and heart?
2. Are your heart qualities apparent to your colleagues, or is it all about your technical competencies?
3. What could you do starting today to illustrate your true heart qualities, the things you really stand for?

Leading well means hiring and promoting for head and heart.

THE SERVANT AS LEADER

ROBERT GREENLEAF

Becoming a servant-leader begins with the natural feeling that one wants to serve, to serve first. Then conscious choice brings one to aspire to lead. That person is sharply different from one who is leader first

...

The difference manifests itself in the care taken by the servant first to make sure that other people's highest priority needs are being served. The best test, and the most difficult to administer, is this: Do those served grow as persons? Do they, while being served, become healthier, wiser, freer, more autonomous, more likely themselves to become servants?

THEME

SERVING

Robert Greenleaf (1904–1990) was the founder of the modern servant leadership movement. He worked for AT&T for forty years, where he spent considerable time researching management and leadership. In the 1970s, he published a series of essays including "The Servant as Leader" from which this excerpt is taken.

I was fortunate in the late 1970s to work for Jan and Olga Erteszek, the owners of an innovative ladies' apparel company. Knowing my interest in leadership, Jan gave me a copy of some of Greenleaf's essays. With a twinkle in his eye, he said, "I think you'll enjoy reading these." The essays changed my view of leadership, and in so doing they changed my life.

Later, in the 1980s, I learned Robert Greenleaf was in an assisted-living facility. June and I drove hundreds of miles to visit him and pay our respects to this giant leadership thinker.

Until I read Greenleaf, my view of leadership was traditional. It was perhaps caring, but was essentially top-down, command-and-control with the leader in charge, knowing the answers, and motivating people to follow him (in this case, me). Maybe in a crisis we need that form of leadership, but it doesn't work on a continual basis.

People may begrudgingly comply with an autocratic commander, but they don't willingly follow. Conversely, as Greenleaf wrote, the power really resides with the followers. They, and only they, will determine if you are a leader or not. They will only willingly follow if they believe you are serving them, helping them grow as persons, becoming healthier, wiser, freer, more autonomous, more likely themselves to become servant leaders.

Sadly, I didn't start out as a serving leader as Robert Greenleaf counseled. Perhaps you didn't either? But it's not too late. I learned, changed my ways, and am so happy I did. It's not too late for you too to become a servant leader.

PRACTICAL APPLICATIONS

1. Do the people you lead believe you are serving them or yourself?
2. What are you currently doing to make them believe that?
3. What can you demonstrate, starting today, to have them realize you are serving them?

Followers bestow leadership on those who serve them.

THE REQUEST OF JAMES AND JOHN

MARK 10: 35-45, THE BIBLE

Then James and John, the sons of Zebedee, came to him. "Teacher," they said, "we want you to do for us whatever we ask."

"'What do you want me to do for you?" he [Jesus] asked.

They replied, "Let one of us sit at your right and the other at your left in your glory."

"You don't know what you are asking," Jesus said. "Can you drink the cup I drink or be baptized with the baptism I am baptized with?"

"We can," they answered.

Jesus said to them, "You will drink the cup I drink and be baptized with the baptism I am baptized with, but to sit at my right or left is not for me to grant. These places belong to those for whom they have been prepared."

When the ten [other apostles] heard about this, they became indignant with James and John. Jesus called them together and said, "You know that those who are regarded as rulers of the Gentiles lord it over them, and their high officials exercise authority over them. Not so with you. Instead, whoever wants to become great among you must be your servant, and whoever wants to be first must be slave of all. For even the Son of Man did not come to be served, but to serve, and to give his life as a ransom for many."

THEME

BEING GREAT BY SERVING

Nobel Peace Prize winner Dr. Martin Luther King, Jr. (1929–1968) was a Baptist minister and leader in the African-American civil rights movement. He advocated nonviolent civil disobedience.

Dr. King spoke the words, "... everybody can be great because everybody can serve..." in a 1968 sermon titled "The Drum Major Instinct."[19] Dr. King's sermon quoted Jesus' words from Mark 10: 35-45: "[He] did not come to be served, but to serve." King cited the deep desire in many of us to be the drum major, leading the parade, being first, strutting proud, high-stepping in front of the glorious marching band with cheering crowds overflowing the streets we cavalcade. This desire is the seduction of our egos.

Many of us don't realize (I didn't for a long while) that greatness is determined by service-service in whatever one chooses to do. Too often, we either seek to be great by calling attention to our own "greatness," an approach that ultimately falls on deaf ears as others observe our vanity. Or, we disempower ourselves, believing only a gifted few can do noble deeds. In our minds saying, "Who am I with all my limitations to believe I can have great impact?"

Yet, history is rife with examples of greatness emanating from humble sources. Look at the greatness of Mother Teresa. Look at the examples of Mahatma Gandhi and Nelson Mandela, both of whom were activist leaders before becoming political leaders. Look at Rosa Parks, the woman who refused to ride at the back of a bus in 1955 amidst racially segregated Alabama. And Alice Paul, a leader more than a century ago in the American suffragette movement. And Helen Keller, who though deaf and blind, wrote twelve books and traveled widely, inspiring others with disabilities to blossom.

All these examples are based on the concept of serving others. Mothers serve, so do fathers, teachers, nurses, taxi drivers, and fire fighters. In the words of Dr. King, all you need is "a heart full of grace and a soul generated by love."

I love author Max De Pree's quote:

The first responsibility of a leader is to define reality.
The last is to say thank you. In between the leader is servant.

PRACTICAL APPLICATIONS

1. Is your mindset one of serving others?

2. To what degree is your heart full of grace and your soul filled with love?

3. What can you do today to begin showing you intend to serve others?

Leading well means understanding your role is to serve others.

SPEAK GENTLY

AUTHOR UNKNOWN

Speak gently,-it is better far
To rule by love than fear;
Speak gently,-let no harsh word mar
The good we may do here.
Speak gently to the young,-for they
Will have enough to bear;
Pass through this life as best they may,
'Tis full of anxious care.
Speak gently to the aged one,
Grieve not the careworn heart;
The sands of life are nearly run,
Let them in peace depart.
Speak gently to the erring ones;
They must have toiled in vain;
Perchance unkindness made them so;
O, win them back again!
Speak gently,-'tis a little thing,
Dropped in the heart's deep well;
The good, the joy, that it may bring,
Eternity shall tell.

THEME

SPEAKING GENTLY

Many scholars attribute the poem "Speak Gently" to David Bates, a nineteenth century American poet. Others attribute it to a nineteenth century British writer, G.W. Hangford. I have been unable to verify the true author.

"Speak Gently" parallels some powerful verse from American author Richelle Goodrich:

When it comes to the crusty behavior of some people, give them the benefit of the doubt. They may be drowning right before your eyes, but you can't see it.

And you'd never ask someone to drown with a smile on his face.

How many times in my hurried life was I not so gentle with the young, or the elderly, or those who had erred? How often did I shout at the person who cut me off in traffic, or raise my voice in irritation?

My father was often angry. He worked diligently at a factory job he hated in order to support us. His health was poor, and he had little education. I may have learned some of my angry ways from his example, so that when I was called out about my anger, my response was, "Well, that's just who I am." Baloney. Anger, like all emotions, floods our senses, but it's up to us to take control of those emotions. This is a learned skill.

"Take a breath, Bob. Count to ten. Walk around the block. Look outside at nature and count your blessings." That's what I should have said to myself.

None of us really know the trials and tribulations other people bear. I remember asking impatiently of someone who had missed a critical meeting why he had been absent before he softly informed me there had been a death in his family. Ouch.

Over the years, I have learned, slowly and painfully, to be more patient, to be more tolerant and understanding. I am far from perfect now with this cross of intensity and impatience that I bear, but I have learned to speak more gently. Progress. I realize now that someone may be drowning before me, and that I can't yet see it.

PRACTICAL APPLICATIONS

1. Could someone you are frustrated with be drowning before your eyes while you can't see it?
2. Do you speak gently to people?
3. Would your leadership be more effective if you did?
4. What habit can you start today to train yourself to speak more gently?

Good leaders have learned to speak more gently.

DISTRUST APPEARANCES

C. J. DENNIS

He came into the bird-shop where I stood
A hulking giant, monumental, grim,
A paragon of muscular manhood.
'What is sold here,' I thought, 'that could serve him?'
His heavy brow, his grat, prognathic [great protruding] jaw
Spoke brooding truculence; he wore no vest;
And, where his shirt flared one side, I saw
The matted hair upon his mighty chest.

I thought of Gog, Carnera [boxers], Hercules,
As he stood by me, breating [breathing] like a gale.
'What can he want,' I wondered, ''mid all these.
Pet dogs, birds, goldfish offered here for sale?
Bulldogs at least.' The parrots watched him, tense;
The yelping pups grew still to see him pass;
All sensed his presence, dominant, immense.
Even the goldfish goggled thro' their glass.

He scared me. Hastily I made my choice
And paid my cash. Yet loitered by the door,
Longing to hear the thinder [thunder] of that voice
Rumble and break into a sudden roar;
Longing to know, amongst these playful folk
Pups, parrots, love-birds-what could be his need.
Sharks? Panthers? ... Then his piping treble [high-pitched musical] spoke:
'Please, miss, three pennorth [pennies worth] of canary seed.

THEME

JUDGING WITHOUT BEING JUDGMENTAL

Clarence Michael James Stanislaus Dennis (1876–1938), better known as C. J. Dennis, was an Australian poet known for his humor. When he died at the age of 61, Australia's prime minister suggested that Dennis was destined to be remembered as the "Australian Robert Burns."[20]

How often do we rush to judgment about a person upon first appearance? Perhaps our limbic brains, hardwired to control our emotions, immediately assesses friend or foe. Or perhaps our pattern-seeking neocortex seeks to classify and pigeonhole something we don't recognize into something we are comfortable with? Too often, we make snap judgments that prove to be wrong.

Matthew 7: 1-3 in the Bible tells us, "Judge not, that ye not be judged," but a further reading of that passage indicates that Jesus abhors hypocritical judgments (observing the mote in your brother's eye, but ignoring the beam in your own eye). We need to avoid being hypocritically judgmental.

Leadership requires judgments in order to make decisions. We judge how a candidate fits with our organization, or the factors involved before deciding to take a certain risk or not. We judge an employee's performance before deciding to give them a small or large raise in pay. Leaders must make such judgments, but must not be hypocritically judgmental, especially not on surface appearances, such as C.J. Davis' observer in the pet shop. That observer judged the new customer based on his facial appearance, body type, and clothes. "How did he belong here?" Yet how wrong the observer was when the customer asked for three pennies worth of canary seed.

I've been judgmental about homeless people I've seen at freeway exits with cardboard signs asking for a handout. I've been judgmental about people speaking with heavily-accented English. I've been judgmental about ostentatiously successful people, musing how they really got to be so successful. "Weren't they just lucky?" I asked myself jealously. Seldom did I pause to find out what their real story was, what hardships they faced, or what trails and tribulations they have borne. I'm still learning how to be less judgmental.

One of the best ways I've found to get to really know people you have just met is to ask them to tell you their story. Where are they from? What about their family? What do they enjoy doing? What are they looking forward to? After a brief, surprised pause, you'd be amazed at what people will tell you about their own personal journeys.

PRACTICAL APPLICATIONS

1. Are you hypocritically judgmental about people?
2. Might it be worthwhile to ask people you work with to tell their "stories"?
3. Perhaps you can start by sharing your own story openly and honestly with them?
4. What three things might you do to avoid snap judgments?
5. Can you put some of those ideas into practice today?

Good leaders make judgments without being superficially judgmental.

DIFFERENCES ARE NOTHING

J.K. ROWLING

Professor Albus Dumbledore:

"I say to you all, once again-in the light of Lord Voldemort's return-we are only as strong as we are united, as weak as we are divided. Lord Voldemort's gift for spreading discord and enmity is very great. We can fight it only by showing an equally strong bond of friendship and trust. Differences of habit and language are nothing at all if our aims are identical and our hearts are open."

THEME

BRIDGING FACTIONS

J.K. Rowling (1965–) is a British novelist whose *Harry Potter* series has sold hundreds of millions of copies. The series chronicles the adventures of Harry Potter and his friends at Hogwarts School of Witchcraft and Wizardry. Their quest is to defeat the evil Dark Lord Voldemort. Professor Dumbledore's words are quoted from *Harry Potter and the Goblet of Fire*.

Too often, we focus on the differences among us and not enough on the common objectives and goals we all share. Enemies seek to divide us, knowing, as U. S. president Abraham Lincoln said in 1858 before the Civil War broke out,

A house divided against itself cannot stand.

Professor Dumbledore knows the importance of friendship and trust, of being strong in unity, and of disregarding differences of habits and language. Great nations often spawn the seeds of their own destruction-think of the Roman, Ottoman, Austro-Hungarian, and Russian empires. Organizations often do the same through dissension within. Internal discord starts with people focusing too much on their differences, pursuing their individual vanities, and not enough on the common purpose, values, and visions they share, which they don't realize are greater than their differences.

All organizations, especially large ones, have factions within them because people naturally form into groups of like-minded people: individuals who share the same background, gender, ethnic culture, religious beliefs, political stances, or views on important issues. These factions are often at odds with each other within the organization. That dissension can be fatal.

As Harvard professors Ron Heifitz and Marty Linsky instructed when I attended the Kennedy School's leadership certification course, "leaders bridge factions." It's difficult. It takes patient, honest, open listening, letting people vent, seeking and finding common ground, avoiding manipulation, and reframing differences over and over again into higher-level areas of agreement.

No one said leadership would be easy. It's all about bringing people together for a higher purpose, not wallowing in differences that are immaterial to the greater good.

PRACTICAL APPLICATIONS

1. What are the factions within your organization?
2. What legitimate viewpoints does each faction hold?
3. How might you bridge these factions to achieve a higher purpose?

Good leaders bridge factions.

THE PLACE WHERE WE ARE RIGHT

YEHUDA AMICHAI

From the place where we are right,
flowers will never grow in the spring.
The place where we are right
is hard and trampled like a yard.
But doubts and loves dig up the world
like a mole, a plow.
And a whisper will be heard in the place
where the ruined house once stood.

THEME

BEING OPEN-MINDED

Yehuda Amichai (1924–2000) was an Israeli poet considered by many in Israel and internationally to be Israel's greatest modern poet. In his short and powerful poem, "The Place Where We Are Right," Amichai speaks of "rightness" and humility.

Where there is self-righteous closed-mindedness, the ground is barren, trampled by stomping feet where people insist on their own version of truth. Nothing grows or blooms there because the ground is stone hard. People are set in their ways, unreceptive to other viewpoints. They are "right." Others are "wrong." Period.

Only where there is honest openness to the views of others, a willingness to actively listen and engage in constructive dialogue for seeking common areas of agreement, and to an attitude of love can there be real growth. That's when the earth is infused with new ideas that fertilize and germinate the seeds waiting there so that new plants can blossom.

Certainly, some core principles can be held in sacred trust: belief in doing the right thing, acting with integrity, seeing the soul in other people, even when they have erred. But one who approaches others with a supercilious attitude such as "I am right, and you are wrong. Let me show you the foolish error of your ways," is self-righteous and doomed to be unpersuasive. Indonesian author Toba Beta said,

Self-righteousness belongs to the narrow-minded.

Perhaps an open mind starts in your heart as just a whisper, but then the newness grows and spreads to overtake the ruined house of your blind and self-defeating self-righteousness.

PRACTICAL APPLICATIONS

1. Are you shutting down the germinating seeds of others with your closed-minded self-righteousness?

2. How would your colleagues rate your open-mindedness? Perhaps lower than your ratings?

3. Maybe you should ask your colleagues to anonymously rate your open-minded-ness?

4. What might you begin to do today to open your mindset?

5. Whom could you ask to help you?

Good leaders make judgments without being superficially judgmental.

SHOUTING'S WORST WAY TO CONDUCT ARGUMENT

SYDNEY J. HARRIS

Thomas Aquinas, who knew more about education and persuasion than almost anybody who ever lived, once said that when you want to convert someone to your view, you go over to where he is standing, take him by the hand (mentally speaking), and guide him to where you want to go.

You don't stand across the room and shout at him. You don't call him a dummy. You don't order him to come over to where you are. You start where he is and work from that position. That's the only way to get him to budge.

THEME

STARTING WHERE THEY ARE

Sydney J. Harris (1917–1986) was an American journalist. He wrote twelve books and his weekday column, "Strictly Personal," was syndicated in approximately 200 newspapers. Harris based this 1973 article about "shouting" on St. Thomas Aquinas (1225–1274), an Italian Catholic priest and an influential philosopher. The Aquinas quote, translated from Latin is,

To convert somebody, go and take them by the hand and guide them.

Many of our leaders today who shout at their adversaries could use this wisdom. Perhaps you're as tired as I am of these blustering tirades? Or as disgusted as I am by leaders bombastically degrading their adversaries, or vowing to crush the competition?

But ask yourself first, "How am I conducting myself in the political argument I got into with my neighbor?" "How am I handling the dialogue with my colleague who gets under my skin?" "How am I dealing with my overly-rebellious teenager who defies our rules intended for their own good?"

It's easy to criticize high-profile leaders for their outrageous behavior. It's much more difficult for us to be civil in our own communications. English writer Mary Wortley Montagu said,

Civility costs nothing but buys everything.

My own process for avoiding bombast and persuading people to change is:

- List the points you agree on with your adversary (you can always find some) and draw a circle around them.
- Find an issue slightly outside that circle of agreement, avoiding those that are far outside, and see if you both can pull that point into the circle of agreement through reasoned dialogue.
- Repeat.
- When you can no longer agree on issues, then agree to respectfully disagree.

PRACTICAL APPLICATIONS

1. Are you willing to mentally walk over to where your adversary stands to understand their point of view?

2. Can you find some common ground where you both agree?

3. Can you then discuss one point where you only slightly disagree to see if you can gain agreement?

4. Even when you disagree with someone, can you do so respectfully?

To get people to follow you, you need to start where they are.

LOVE ALL, TRUST A FEW

WILLIAM SHAKESPEARE

Be thou blest, Bertram, and succeed thy father
In manners, as in shape! thy blood and virtue
Contend for empire in thee, and thy goodness
Share with thy birthright!
Love all, trust a few, Do wrong to none ...

THEME

LEARNING TO TRUST

William Shakespeare (1564–1616) wrote this advice from a countess to her son in Act 1, Scene 1, of his play *All's Well That Ends Well*. Many of us have had our trust violated, oftentimes by someone close to us. Our natural tendency then is to withhold trust, bestowing it only on a few friends, some family members, or close colleagues. That's a mistake.

Early in my career, I became the CEO of a small firm owned by some venture capitalists. We tripled the business in a few years, and I was intent on seeing the company sell its shares in the public market. One day I was summoned to the venture capital offices one hundred miles away and told they had sold the company to a large firm. I was outraged by their decision and the fact I was never even consulted. After the deal closed, I had a chip on my shoulder and acted like an immature, disgruntled jerk to the new owners. Before long, they fired me, appointing one of the VPs who had previously reported to me as the new CEO. I was deeply hurt and embarrassed, especially after I learned the new owners had talked to the VPs behind my back about who should succeed me. I felt betrayed. My trust had been broken.

Then somewhere I read or heard, "Love many and trust few, and always paddle your own canoe." I can't recall the author, but the verse resonated with me. I wouldn't trust so openly in the future. I'd withhold trust and just operate independently.

Slowly, I learned that an untrusting attitude just doesn't work. My lack of trust emanated from my body language and my eyes. People in turn didn't trust me. My leadership suffered as a result. Of course some people are untrustworthy, so we must be cautious when dealing with them. Our world has liars and cheats, who, unfortunately, are quick to take advantage of others.

Most people, however, the vast majority in my experience, are trustworthy, and trust needs to be solidified and built up with them. From mutual trust, the relationships so essential to leadership can be built. I painfully learned that to lead I must overcome my fears, take some measured risks, and learn to trust most people again.

Shakespeare's Countess was wrong. We must love all and trust many, not just a few.

PRACTICAL APPLICATIONS

1. Are you afraid to trust?

2. Is that attitude working well for you?

3. What might you do today to extend some trust to others?

Good leaders overcome their fear to trust.

BELIEF VERSUS TRUST

GAN CHENNAI

Belief is Doubtful, Trust is Certain

Belief is from Mind, Trust is from Heart

Belief is Lip Service; Trust is Heart Felt

Believe many; Trust only a Few

Believing is Easy, Trusting is Hard

Belief scores 50%, Trust scores 100%

Belief is Ordinary; Trust is Extra-ordinary

Belief is Start point; Trust is End Point

Belief is Limited; Trust is infinite

Belief is Shaking Hands, Trust is Embracing

Belief keeps Control; Trust gives up control

Belief is jumping opportunities; Trust is staying

Belief is not Time Tested; Trust passes Tough Times

Belief is Partial; Trust is Complete

Believe in Thoughts; Trust your Intuition

Belief in God is Attempting; Trust in God is Surrender

Belief is Important; Trust is Essential

Belief is Plastic Rose; Trust is Real Rose.

THEME

BELIEVING VERSUS TRUSTING

Gan Chennai (1961–), a pen name, is a senior technical officer at the Central Electronics Engineering Research Institute in India. He writes free verse poetry as a hobby and for his own spiritual evolution.

Chennai's poem depicts the power of trust, comparing it to belief. Belief can be powerful, but trust takes human relationships to a deeper level. Belief emerges from our logical minds, but trust plumbs a deeper level, something closer to the soul. Trust involves some risk of being taken advantage of. But showing through your words and body language that you don't trust someone guarantees the self-fulfilling prophecy that you won't be trusted back.

Leadership-experts Jim Kouzes and Barry Posner wrote that "leaders go first" in extending trust to others. So true. Leaders extend what author Stephen M. R. Covey calls "smart trust," beginning with a modicum of trust and then building more or less trust depending on the other person's behavior. Trust is built when someone is vulnerable but not taken advantage of.

Leadership is all about relationships, so trust is essential. We may not understand more esoteric concepts like "ethical" (who defines what's right?) or "values-based relationships" (whose values?), but we inherently understand trust because we experience it (or the lack of it) every day with family or colleagues.

For several years I have been associated with Trust Across America-Trust Around the World (TAA-TAW), an organization whose mission is to help organizations build trust. We have published several books under the *Trust Inc.* title. Each year TAA-TAW names North America's most trustworthy organizations and the top thought leaders in trust. (I'm honored to be named as one of those thought leaders for the past several years.) Included in this list is my friend Bob Whipple, known as the "Trust Ambassador," whom I admire so much. Some of Bob's keen insights are quoted shortly.

Trust is a powerful force in building strong relationships. Trust trumps belief.

PRACTICAL APPLICATIONS

1. Do your colleagues trust that you have their back?
2. Is there someone to whom you can extend trust to enhance your relationship?
3. What might you do today to show more trust in your colleagues?

Good leaders go first in building smart trust with people.

THE CREMATION OF SAM MCGEE

ROBERT SERVICE

There are strange things done in the midnight sun
By the men who moil [work hard] for gold;
The Arctic trails have their secret tales
That would make your blood run cold;
The Northern Lights have seen queer sights,
But the queerest they ever did see
Was that night on the marge of Lake Lebarge
I cremated Sam McGee.

Now Sam McGee was from Tennessee, where the cotton blooms and blows.
Why he left his home in the South to roam 'round the Pole, God only knows.
He was always cold, but the land of gold seemed to hold him like a spell;
Though he'd often say in his homely way that "he'd sooner live in hell."
...
And that very night, as we lay packed tight in our robes beneath the snow,
And the dogs were fed, and the stars o'erhead were dancing heel and toe,
He turned to me, and "Cap," says he, "I'll cash in this trip, I guess;
And if I do, I'm asking that you won't refuse my last request."
Well, he seemed so low that I couldn't say no; then he says with a sort of moan:
"It's the cursèd cold, and it's got right hold, till I'm chilled clean through to the bone.
Yet 'tain't being dead-it's my awful dread of the icy grave that pains;
So I want you to swear that, foul or fair, you'll cremate my last remains."
...
Now a promise made is a debt unpaid, and the trail has its own stern code.
In the days to come, though my lips were dumb, in my heart how I cursed that load.
...
Till I came to the marge [edge] of Lake Lebarge, and a derelict [abandoned ship] there lay;
It was jammed in the ice, but I saw in a trice [quickly] it was called the "Alice May."
And I looked at it, and I thought a bit, and I looked at my frozen chum;
Then "Here," said I, with a sudden cry, "is my cre-ma-tor-eum."
Some planks I tore from the cabin floor, and I lit the boiler fire;
Some coal I found that was lying around, and I heaped the fuel higher;
The flames just soared, and the furnace roared-such a blaze you seldom see;
And I burrowed a hole in the glowing coal, and I stuffed in Sam McGee.
...
I was sick with dread, but I bravely said: "I'll just take a peep inside.
I guess he's cooked, and it's time I looked"; ... then the door I opened wide.
And there sat Sam, looking cool and calm, in the heart of the furnace roar;
And he wore a smile you could see a mile, and said: "Please close that door.
It's fine in here, but I greatly fear, you'll let in the cold and storm-
Since I left Plumtree, down in Tennessee, it's the first time I've been warm."

THEME

KEEPING YOUR PROMISES

Robert Service (1874–1958) was a British-Canadian bank clerk and poet often called the "Bard of the Yukon" for his vivid portrayals of the Klondike gold rush.[21] He published "The Cremation of Sam McGee" in 1907.

This comic verse is all about keeping your promises, even though it may be extremely difficult. Good leaders not only hold people accountable to keep their promised commitments, they are also keenly aware of their own responsibilities as a leader. Good leaders don't pass the buck, scapegoat others, and avoid responsibility. Good leaders look in their mirrors asking how much of the current situation is their responsibility. Then good leaders step up and take the heat, showing some vulnerability in the process.

My friend Bob Whipple, the "Trust Ambassador," had a distinguished career in corporate America building teams, developing leaders, and learning about the critical importance of trust to leadership. Now Bob writes and speaks around the world on how to build trust. Building trust is a complex subject, as Bob is quick to point out. One of the most critical dimensions of leadership is understanding one's responsibilities and keeping one's explicit and implicit commitments.

Bob wrote an article in 2011 titled "Leaders: Hold Yourself Accountable."[22] In it he presents a hypothetical case for a plant manager suffering with low morale in his factory. His supervisors tell him the workers are upset by the absence of raises and the threat of layoffs. Productivity is low, and costs are high. Is a workforce reduction demanded to increase profitability, as many mangers would think?

Bob asks the manager to look in the mirror and answer some tough questions:

- How have you been contributing to this problem?
- What are you accountable for in this situation?
- Who else have you been passing the blame to?
- What behaviors do you need to change to build trust with the workforce?
- What new assistance might you need to solve these issues?

Yes, it's uncomfortable to confront these questions, admitting you are a part of the problem too. Even in my turnaround experience when I was supposed to have all the right answers, I often found that I, too, had to admit after a while that I was a part of the problem as well. Then people really opened up. Good leaders both hold people accountable for their commitments and understand their own responsibilities as leaders.

PRACTICAL APPLICATIONS

1. Are you keeping your promises, even though the commitments are difficult?
2. Are you scapegoating others?
3. What might you do starting today to keep your promises?

Good leaders keep their explicit and implicit promises.

TAO TE CHING

LAO-TZU

A leader is best when people barely know that he exists,

not so good when people obey and acclaim him,

worst when they despise him.

Fail to honor people,

They fail to honor you.

But of a good leader, who talks little,

when his work is done, his aims fulfilled,

they will all say,

"We did this ourselves."

THEME

ELEVATING OTHER PEOPLE

The Tao is an ancient Chinese belief system sometimes called The Way or The Path. The Tao is the fundamental text for Taoism, which emphasizes living in harmony with The Way. The teachings of the Tao began with a philosopher and poet named Lao-Tzu, who wrote sometime between the sixth and fourth centuries BCE.

The Tao contains many chapters of verse and many different translations of those verses exist. This translation of the Chapter 17 poem from the Tao about how "A leader is best" deals with the various types of leaders. People fear some leaders, only begrudgingly complying with their edicts, fearfully obeying but not willingly following.

According to Lao-Tzu, the best leader is quiet and humble, working for the good of the group so that they feel proud of their mutual accomplishments. The best leader honors people and is, therefore, honored in return. Leading this way, people feel liberated, unleashed, empowered, and pleased with what they have accomplished together. For Lao-Tzu, it's not about you, the leader; it's all about *them*, the people you lead.

In many areas, we have it all wrong. Take public speaking for example. Most novice speakers are hung up on how to look good, be eloquent, and have a stage presence that's just right. Such concerns lead to disconnect with an audience because people sense the speaker is too self-absorbed. A great speaker takes the mindset that it's all about them, the audience. The speaker and the leader must be wholeheartedly there for "them." This insight took me years to understand, but it's a lesson that has made all the difference.

PRACTICAL APPLICATIONS

1. Is it all about, or mostly about, you? Your title, your position, your pay, your perquisites, your power, your persona? You, you, you?

2. Do people just begrudgingly comply, obeying your edicts, dragging their feet and mumbling under their breath?

3. Are you feared as a leader? (That's the worst.)

4. Make a short list of a few things you might start doing today to shift your mindset to honor and elevate "them."

Leading people well is about elevating and honoring others so they can feel "we did this ourselves."

WE WHO HAVE LIVED IN CONCENTRATION CAMPS

VICTOR FRANKL

We who have lived in concentration camps can remember the men who walked through the huts comforting others, giving away their last piece of bread. They may have been few in number, but they offer sufficient proof that everything can be taken from man but one thing: the last of the human freedoms-to choose one's attitude in any given set of circumstances-to choose one's own way.

THEME

CHOOSING YOUR ATTITUDE

Viktor Frankl (1905–1997) wrote these words in his seminal book, *Man's Search for Meaning*, published in 1946. During World War II, the Nazis imprisoned Frankl, a Jewish-Austrian neurologist and psychiatrist, at a series of concentration camps including Auschwitz. He discovered the importance of meaning in life, and thus found a reason to continue living, even after his wife, mother, and brother died in the camps.[23]

Frankl further wrote in *Man's Search for Meaning*:

… for the first time in my life I saw the truth as it is set into song by so many poets, proclaimed as the final wisdom by so many thinkers. The truth-that love is the ultimate and the highest goal to which Man can aspire. Then I grasped the meaning of the greatest secret that human poetry and human thought and belief have to impart:
The salvation of Man is through love and in love.

The lesson here is that, no matter the suffering and atrocities one incurs, one can choose one's attitude and turn to what Frankl learns is the ultimate truth: love.

When a few starving and tortured men in an unspeakable concentration camp walk around to comfort other prisoners and give away their last pieces of bread, it is an act of love that derives from the last of their human freedoms: "To choose one's attitude in any given set of circumstances…." The evils the Nazis committed were powerless against such a force for good.

I choose an attitude of optimism and love. I choose to believe there is more good in people than bad. I choose to believe that, in spite of all the horrors of the last century, our world is getting better. Nobel-Prize winner, Angus Deaton, says in his book *The Great Escape: Health, Wealth, and the Origins of Inequality*, more people live longer today and have a better quality of life, and the number of people in extreme poverty has fallen from 84 percent to 24 percent from 1820 to 1992.[24] I maintain a positive outlook on life.

What kind of attitude defines your outlook on life?

PRACTICAL APPLICATIONS

1. In your current circumstances, what attitude do you choose to take?

2. Does your attitude reflect enduring your sufferings in a noble and honorable way?

3. Can you be comforting and loving to others, even giving away your last piece of bread?

4. If not, maybe it's time for you to undertake an attitude adjustment?

Leading well means choosing an optimistic, loving attitude regardless of the circumstances.

THE PRINCE

NICCOLO MACHIAVELLI

And let it be noted that there is no more delicate matter to take in hand, nor more dangerous to conduct, nor more doubtful in its success, than to set up as the leader in the introduction of changes. For he who innovates will have for his enemies all those who are well off under the existing order of things, and only lukewarm supporters in those who might be better off under the new.

THEME

CHALLENGING THE STATUS QUO

Niccolo di Bernardo di Machiavelli (1469–1527) was an Italian historian, politician, and writer. He was an official in the Florentine Republic and wrote *The Prince* in 1513 in which he extolled the importance of a powerful ruler who was not afraid to be harsh with his subjects and enemies, even if it meant acting unethically to protect his power. So many poor leaders today from Wall Street to Washington to the C-suites of corporations worldwide think Machiavelli was right and that we have to lead his way in today's world. They're wrong.

While virtually all good leaders today reject Machiavelli's ideas about the unethical use of power, we can agree with him that there is likely no more difficult an undertaking than to initiate a paradigm change. The critics will be vocal and prolific.

There's an old adage about frogs being comfortable in a pot, even if the temperature is slowly rising. The frogs stay put because the change is happening slowly, unnoticed. They don't jump out, and ultimately the frogs boil to death. So it is with people confronted with the prospect of having to make a major change, a jump out of their pot. They stay as the heat rises. Even those frogs/people who suspect they may be better off in a new pot are still unsure if this is the time to leap. They equivocate, "Maybe we should wait and get more information?"

Managers differ from leaders in that managers plan, organize, budget, and control within their existing pots. Leaders serve people by encouraging them to jump to a better pot, where they then regroup and jump again, and then again. It's risky and difficult, but it's what leaders do, embracing and propagating change. If you're not leading change, then you're not leading, you're managing inside your current pot.

Leaders face disagreement with and questions about their strategy, tactics, and, worst of all, their intentions, such as accusations of personal motives for self-aggrandizement. I've heard all those carping criticisms during my career. The self-aggrandizement criticisms hurt the most because I knew my intentions were honorable, but I persisted in spite of the critics.

The only way to pursue necessary and positive change is to be confident enough with the critical trust and support of honorable colleagues to persist in what is right, not for you, but for *them*, the people Even then, remaining humble and open.

PRACTICAL APPLICATIONS

1. What new pot might you set the sights of your group on?
2. Are you ready to endure the inevitable criticism to do some good for the people you serve?
3. Then proceed with confident resolve.

Good leaders challenge the status quo.

INAUGURAL ADDRESS

FRANKLIN DELANO ROOSEVELT

... This is preeminently the time to speak the truth, the whole truth, frankly and boldly. Nor need we shrink from honestly facing conditions in our country today. This great Nation will endure as it has endured, will revive and will prosper. So, first of all, let me assert my firm belief that the only thing we have to fear is fear itself-nameless, unreasoning, unjustified terror which paralyzes needed efforts to convert retreat into advance. In every dark hour of our national life a leadership of frankness and vigor has met with that understanding and support of the people themselves which is essential to victory

....

We face the arduous days that lie before us in the warm courage of the national unity; with the clear consciousness of seeking old and precious moral values; with the clean satisfaction that comes from the stern performance of duty by old and young alike

....

The people of the United States have not failed. In their need they have registered a mandate that they want direct, vigorous action. They have asked for discipline and direction under leadership. They have made me the present instrument of their wishes. In the spirit of the gift I take it

....

THEME

VIGOROUS ACTION IN ADVERSITY

The inauguration of Franklin Delano Roosevelt (1882–1945) as the 32nd president of the United States was held on March 4, 1933. It was a time of crisis in the country with widespread unemployment, bankruptcies, and bank failures. People everywhere were wondering what had happened and what could be done. The Great Depression was unprecedented in its scope and depth, calling for unprecedented responses.

The day after his inauguration, Roosevelt assembled a special session of Congress, declaring a four-day bank holiday. He then signed the Emergency Banking Act, providing a mechanism for reopening banks. In his First 100 Days of his "New Deal" and subsequently, FDR implemented a series of pioneering actions referred to as the "3 R's," relief, recovery, and reform. The relief was for the unemployed and poor. The recovery was for the economy. The reform was to prevent a recurrence of such a devastating downswing.[25]

In his 1933 inaugural address, as he prepared to undertake these burdensome tasks, FDR honestly and frankly faced reality, not trying to sugarcoat the situation. Good leaders acknowledge reality but do so with confidence. Then he pivots in this historic speech to what he knows must be addressed head-on: fear. His stirring words,

… the only thing we have to fear is fear itself-nameless, unreasoning, unjustified terror which paralyzes needed efforts to convert retreat into advance…

In *Triple Crown Leadership*, Gregg and I advocated for the establishment of psychological stability before the turnaround of a company (or in FDR's case of an entire economy) can be established. People can't think and act rationally when they are paralyzed by fear. A vigorous leader like Roosevelt needed to lift that veil of terror blanketing the minds of Americans to stop their mental retreat and to advance them psychologically.

Roosevelt called for courage, "precious moral values," and stern performance of duty. Bridging from the reality of the abyss being faced, he confidently declares that this great nation would endure, revive, and prosper. To do so, direct and vigorous action, discipline, and direction would be needed. Whether you agree with Roosevelt's New Deal policies or not, there is no doubt he was a bold and fearless leader in daunting times.

PRACTICAL APPLICATIONS

1. If people are fearful in your organization, what can you say and do today to lighten their concerns?
2. If your organization is facing a crisis, what vigorous action can you begin to take today to address the issues?
3. What positive vision can you create for your team that puts their focus on a better future?

Good leaders take vigorous action in adversity.

INAUGURAL ADDRESS

JOHN F. KENNEDY

... Let the word go forth from this time and place, to friend and foe alike, that the torch has been passed to a new generation of Americans-born in this century, tempered by war, disciplined by a hard and bitter peace, proud of our ancient heritage-and unwilling to witness or permit the slow undoing of those human rights to which this nation has always been committed, and to which we are committed today at home and around the world.

Let every nation know, whether it wishes us well or ill, that we shall pay any price, bear any burden, meet any hardship, support any friend, oppose any foe to assure the survival and the success of liberty.

....

Now the trumpet summons us again-not as a call to bear arms, though arms we need-not as a call to battle, though embattled we are-but a call to bear the burden of a long twilight struggle, year in and year out, "rejoicing in hope, patient in tribulation"-a struggle against the common enemies of man: tyranny, poverty, disease and war itself

....

And so, my fellow Americans: ask not what your country can do for you-ask what you can do for your country. My fellow citizens of the world: ask not what America will do for you, but what together we can do for the freedom of man. Finally, whether you are citizens of America or citizens of the world, ask of us here the same high standards of strength and sacrifice which we ask of you. With a good conscience our only sure reward, with history the final judge of our deeds, let us go forth to lead the land we love, asking His blessing and His help, but knowing that here on earth God's work must truly be our own.

THEME

CHALLENGING OTHERS TO HIGHER STANDARDS

The inauguration of John F. Kennedy (1917–1963) as the 35th president of the United States was held on January 20, 1961 in Washington, D.C. When he was assassinated in November 1963, I was a senior in college, and my new bride, June, was working as a legal secretary in town to support us. When we heard the shocking news of his death, we dashed to Washington in our blue VW beetle to see the funeral cortege. It was one of the most solemn and moving experiences of our lives.

JFK's 1961 inaugural address is one of the most stirring speeches of the twentieth century. He vividly paints a new vision for America during the dangerous Cold War years with the Soviet Union. He cites traditional American values of freedom and liberty and sends a stern warning of our collective willingness to bear the burdens of a long struggle. As a former young senator from Massachusetts, it was important for Kennedy to announce that he represented a new generation of Americans, strong and resolved to lead the country well.

But to me the most telling aspect of his speech was his reversal of what had been conventional wisdom to many up until then:

Ask not what your country can do for you-ask what you can do for your country.

From the Great Depression of the 1930's and after the end of World War II, the American public grew more used to the government playing a larger role in our lives, passing new laws and regulations, necessary as social safety nets and to curb apparent abuses, but also creating the expectation that big government would continually do more and more to take care of people. As a candidate from the Democratic Party, generally more left of center than the Republicans, it might have been expected that more promises would be made by Kennedy for additional largesse to flow from Washington to the people.

Strikingly, Kennedy declares the opposite. He puts out a clarion trumpet call, summoning people to give, not just get; to serve, not just be served. When I heard his stirring words, I was deeply impressed. Here was a leader not afraid to challenge the conventional wisdom.

Kennedy acknowledged the realities facing America; he issued stern warnings to our adversaries; he called on all Americans to give to and for their country; and he summoned citizens of the world to hold him and us to the same high standards he asked of them. What a wonderful beginning for his presidency.

PRACTICAL APPLICATIONS

1. Are you brave enough in your leadership to challenge the conventional wisdom most people embrace?
2. Are you willing to challenge people to step up to their own responsibilities?
3. What might you do today to constructively ask people to do more?

Good leaders challenge others to higher standards.

COME TO THE EDGE

CHRISTOPHER LOGUE

"Come to the edge."
"We might fall."
"Come to the edge."
"It's too high."
"COME TO THE EDGE."
And they came.
And he pushed.
And they flew.

THEME

PUSHING PEOPLE

"Come to the Edge" by Englishman Christopher Logue (1926–2011) was written in the 1960s for an exhibition of another poet, Guillaume Apollinaire, to whom it is often misattributed. It speaks volumes in only 27 words, and I have long been fascinated by it.

Leadership often means venturing out into the unknown, beyond the comfortable boundaries that everyone knows. Such a venture is risky. It's easier to stay inside the known box because we know how to deal with the challenges in our boxes. People often lament that "Outside the box, in the unknown, we may not be capable of coping. We may not survive, or we may have to learn new survival skills. It's challenging."

Yes, striving together through the unknown is not easy. It's downright scary at times. In certain instances, given enough incentive or great pain in their current situation, a group may overcome their fears and venture forth toward change. More often, though, the group *should* be in a different place, but remains within, paralyzed by the fear of change.

Then the leader must guide the group to the edge. If the leader is trusted, if the group members believe the leader serves them, they will come. Even right to the precipitous edge where the leader may then need to give them a push. Then they discover what he leader already knew: they can fly.

One of the benefits I've gained from working in challenging situations in many different industries is the realization that a team of good people placed into a seemingly impossible situation can know, really know, they can find their way through and out. It may be tough; there may have to be a push or two; there may even be some casualties; but together they can do it and soar. What an incredible, life-changing feeling that is to experience breaking through boundaries with others.

PRACTICAL APPLICATIONS

1. Is your group caught in a constraining box?
2. Are they willing to break out to a completely new place?
3. What might you do today to build more trust into your leadership?
4. Do you believe in them enough to give them a push?

Leading well sometimes means calling people to the edge and giving them a push to discover they can fly.

LESSONS FROM THE GEESE

DR. ROBERT MCNEISH

As each goose flying in formation flaps its wings, it creates an "uplift" for the bird following. By flying in a "V," the whole flock adds 71 percent more flying range than if each bird flew alone.

Whenever a goose falls out of formation, it suddenly feels the drag and resistance of trying to fly alone, and quickly gets back into formation to take advantage of the "lifting power" of the bird immediately in front.

When the lead goose gets tired, it rotates back into the formation and another goose flies at the point position.

The geese in formation honk from behind to encourage those up front to keep up their speed.

When a goose gets sick or wounded or shot down, two geese drop out of formation and follow their fellow member down to help provide protection. They stay with this member of the flock until he or she is either able to fly again or dies. Then they launch out on their own, with another formation, or catch up with their own flock.

THEME

WORKING TOGETHER

Dr. Robert McNeish, a science teacher and administrator in Baltimore, wrote these curious verses in 1972. Here are the lessons Dr. McNeish cited in his "Lessons from Geese":

People who share a common direction and sense of community can get
where they are going quicker and easier because they are traveling on the
thrust of each another.
If we have as much sense as a goose, we will join in formations with those who are
headed where we want to go.
It pays to take turns doing the hard tasks and sharing leadership-
with people, as with geese, interdependent with one another.
We need to make sure our honking from behind is encouraging-
not something less helpful.
If we have as much sense as the geese, we'll stand by each other like that.

During my business career, I experienced groups traveling on the forward thrust of one another because we were aligned. (In *Triple Crown Leadership*, we devoted a whole chapter on how to align an organization.) I saw leaders emerge from the group, take on a leadership task, and then continue to lead on other tasks, or step back as a follower. I experienced a lot of shared leadership where hierarchical leaders encouraged others to lead and, hopefully, succeed, or even fail gently in order to learn from the experience. I heard a lot of positive honking as we encouraged each other. Moreover, I saw us care for each other.

Most impressive, when we applied the lessons learned from the geese, we accomplished incredible results together.

PRACTICAL APPLICATIONS

1. Do you share a common direction and sense of community with your colleagues?
2. Are you aligned in formation with your colleagues?
3. Are you sharing in the difficult tasks and letting others lead at times?
4. Do you honk encouragement?
5. Do you come in to help your colleagues in trouble?
6. If you're not pleased with your answers, what can you do, starting now, to improve?

Leading well means working together, sharing leadership, and encouraging each other.

LOVE IS PATIENT

1 CORINTHIANS, 13: 4-8

Love is patient, love is kind.

It does not envy, it does not boast, it is not proud.

It is not rude. It is not self-seeking.

It is not easily angered. It keeps no record of wrongs.

Love does not delight in evil.

But rejoices with the truth.

It always protects, always trusts, always hopes, always perseveres.

Love never fails.

THEME

ANCHORING IN LOVE

We should be willing to use the word "love" in our work settings. We know love goes beyond physical attraction. Love exists between family members and close friends, and it includes what we feel for those first responders who put their lives on the line for us, as well as what soldiers feel for their comrades in battle. The Greek word "agape" describes brotherly love and charity, separating it from "eros" indicating intimate love.

Love can be a deep personal bond between people, a trusting relationship. Caring for another person, compassion, respect, and appreciation for others are all expressions of love. As leadership author Tommy Spaulding says in his new book *The Heart-Led Leader*:

Leading from the heart means leading with love. If the word love scares you, then use passion, commitment, compassion, servant leadership, purpose-driven, mission-driven, or your choice of any similar word or phrase, because at the core these are all forms of love.

Love knows that evil can't be trusted. Evil lies. Love protects others, especially those who are vulnerable. Love trusts first, like leaders trust first, and then builds more or less trust from there. Love builds hope for a brighter future and perseveres to create that future.

Your leadership will be rooted in either love or fear. It's up to you to choose which to use as your anchor.

PRACTICAL APPLICATIONS

1. Write down today which of these are too prevalent in your life:
   a. Impatience? Envy? Boastfulness? Excessive pride?
   b. Have you been rude? Self-seeking?
   c. Are you easily angered, keeping mental records of wrongs?
   d. Are you loving, compassionate, willing to help and serve others?
2. Write down what you can do today to:
   a. Protect someone, especially someone vulnerable,
   b. Extend someone some trust,
   c. Give someone more hope.
3. Then make a list of how you can persevere in these acts of love more permanently.

Leading well means anchoring your behavior in love.

LOVE AND COMPASSION

THE 14TH DALAI LAMA

... we cannot escape the necessity of love and compassion.

This, then, is my true religion, my simple faith.

In this sense, there is no need for temple or church, for mosque or synagogue,

no need for complicated philosophy, doctrine or dogma.

Our own heart, our mind, is the temple.

The doctrine is compassion.

Love for others and respect for their rights and dignity,

no matter who or what they are:

ultimately, these are all we need.

THEME

CONNECTING WITH YOUR SOUL

The current and 14th Dalai Lama, Tenzin Gyatso (1950–), is a monk in the Gelug school of Tibetan Buddhism. His remarks about love and compassion were published in 1999 in his book *Ethics for the New Millennium*. He travels widely, speaking and writing often about the philosophy of love and compassion, polar opposites to fear and self-centeredness in the context of leadership.

I have learned first-hand over the years that leaders sometimes get it wrong, leading based on fear, power, control, and looking out for themselves. That philosophy is driven by the ego in our minds, which seeks to protect us, and it is also driven by the fight or flight instincts rooted in our DNA through our limbic system (a complex set of brain structures that control our emotions, motivations, and behavior).

Too much of leadership and management today is driven by this command-and-control, top-down, hierarchical-pyramidal structure that is ultimately about fear, control, reward, and punishment. Remember my early goal out of graduate school? It was "I want to run something." My approach was all about me: me in control; me in charge; feeding my ego. As I reflect on it now, all I can think is "Ugh."

In the words of my friend Chuck Wachendorfer,

Your ego is not your amigo.

The Dalai Lama's focus on love and compassion puts us in touch with our souls, which transcend the ego-mind and body, and which in my view connect us with a higher level of universal consciousness we might call God. That soul can be accessed through prayer, meditation, mindfulness, sanctuary, nature, and in leadership at your work through deep connections with the souls of other people.

PRACTICAL APPLICATIONS

1. Are you primarily ego driven, or soul driven?
2. What might you begin to do today to better connect with your soul?

Good leaders are compassionate.

A HAIKU–LEADERSHIP

DEMAS W. JASPER

A true leader leads by example.

Many are led, but
There are men I would die for,
Their cause is so just.

I won't follow one
Who can't set the example.
Leaders are out front.

Charisma is good
In a worthy cause today,
But can mislead us.

Respect comes first though
I'd like to like the leader.
But how safe is he?

Has he thought it through?
Is he truthful, honest, fair?
Will he make it worse?

Can he get me there,
And safely home again, too?
Others count on me.

Not just a grand plan!
Spell it out for me to know.
What sacrifice then?

I want to know now;
Does it serve the common good?
Is it important?

Selfless leadership
Takes courage and "will to win."
Lead me, but lead true.

THEME

LEADING TRUE

Demas W. Jasper (1935–) is an American author, editor, and photographer. He recently published his third book, *Haiku American Style.* Haiku is a Japanese poetic form consisting of seventeen syllables often published in English in three lines of five, seven, and five syllables respectively. Japanese Haiku traditionally juxtaposes two images or ideas.[26] Jasper's Haiku deals with human traits.

In "A Haiku-Leadership," Jasper uses the traditional five, seven, and five syllables on the three lines, but writes a longer passage on the nature of leadership. Jasper has captured the essence of leadership well: working for just causes; serving the common good; leading by example; being respectful, truthful, selfless, and fair; showing courage and will.

Bill George, formerly CEO of Medtronic and now a Harvard Business School professor, has written extensively on these subjects in his books *Authentic Leadership* and *Discover Your True North.* An authentic leader is one who brings people together around a shared purpose and empowers them to create value for others while being true to themselves and what they believe. Good leaders have an internal "true north," a moral compass that guides them, especially through the necessary crucible events of life that test and shape their character. Your true north is composed of your values and principles (north), sweet spot (east), support team (south), and integrated life (west) to arrive at your center of self-awareness. George speaks of being vulnerable to others, and that if you are open and vulnerable to others, how can anyone say something about you that you haven't already revealed? In such vulnerability there is power: not the power to dominate, but the power to build lasting relationships.

The dimensions of authentic leadership are purpose, values, relationships, self-discipline, and heart. These dimensions manifest themselves in characteristics like passion, good behavior, connectedness, consistency, and compassion.

Jasper is willing to be led, but only if he is "led true." Don't you feel the same way?

PRACTICAL APPLICATIONS

1. Do you have an internal compass pointing you toward a noble true north?
2. Are you an authentic leader, true to your own character with a respectful belief in other people?
3. How could you improve your authenticity and moral compass to lead true?

Leading well means being an authentic leader with a "true north" moral compass.

BAND OF BROTHERS

WILLIAM SHAKESPEARE

That he which hath no stomach to this fight,
Let him depart; his passport [passage] shall be made,
And crowns for convoy put into his purse;
We would not die in that man's company
That fears his fellowship to die with us.
This day is call'd the feast of Crispian.
He that outlives this day, and comes safe home,
Will stand a tip-toe when this day is nam'd,
And rouse him at the name of Crispian.
He that shall live this day, and see old age,
Will yearly on the vigil feast his neighbours,
And say "Tomorrow is Saint Crispian."
Then will he strip his sleeve and show his scars,
And say "These wounds I had on Crispin's day."
Old men forget; yet all shall be forgot,
But he'll remember, with advantages,
What feats he did that day. Then shall our names,
Familiar in his mouth as household words-
...
Be in their flowing cups freshly rememb'red.
This story shall the good man teach his son;
And Crispin Crispian shall ne'er go by,
From this day to the ending of the world,
But we in it shall be remembered-
We few, we happy few, we band of brothers;
For he today that sheds his blood with me
Shall be my brother; be he ne'er so vile,
This day shall gentle his condition;
And gentlemen in England now-a-bed
Shall think themselves accurs'd they were not here,
And hold their manhoods cheap whiles any speaks
That fought with us upon Saint Crispian's day.

THEME

CREATING BONDS

William Shakespeare (1564–1616) wrote his powerful play *Henry V* in the late 1590s. A portion of the play depicts Shakespeare's interpretation of the Battle of Agincourt that King Henry V and a small English army fought against a much larger French army in 1415. Amazingly, the English prevailed with Henry himself participating in hand-to-hand combat alongside his men.[27] In Shakespeare's account, King Henry rouses his men by expressing his confidence they would triumph and that the "band of brothers" fighting that day would be able to boast each year on St Crispian's day (a celebration of the birthday of two Christian saints) of their glorious battle.

Shakespeare's phrase "band of brothers" has since been used to rouse other troops in battle, has been the subject of book titles, films, and even an HBO mini-series based on Stephen Ambrose's 1993 book *Band of Brothers* about the 101st Airborne division of the U.S. Army. Influential British Rear-Admiral Horatio Nelson, well known as an inspirational leader, referred to the captains under his command prior to the battle of the Nile in 1798 as a "band of brothers."

What's unusual about Shakespeare's "band of brothers" phrase is that such a plea for fighting alongside the king as a brother was most unusual for the time. Kings were in a much different social class than the troops, and Henry's rousing inspiration coalesced everyone into a cohesive band. King Henry bonded with his troops, pledging that those few who shed their blood with him that day would be his brothers-a remarkable leadership statement for the time. Is it any wonder that the outnumbered troops flung themselves into this battle and emerged victorious?

My experience with leadership echoes Shakespeare's writing. Great leadership is a shared experience. The leadership mantle ebbs and flows between different people depending on their expertise and passion as well as the circumstances. Sometimes the hierarchical leader leads; sometime another leads with the willing assent of the person at the top of the pyramid.

Thus, the dynamic for good leadership is a band of leaders-brothers and sisters-bonded together.

PRACTICAL APPLICATIONS

1. Do you lead from the front or from the safety of the command post in the rear?
2. Do you create a "band of brothers" (regardless of gender) among your colleagues?
3. What might you say, starting today, to create this sense of common purpose, kinship, and camaraderie?

Inspiring leadership creates "bands of brothers" among colleagues.

WISDOM OF THE ELDERS

AUTHOR UNKNOWN

There is a river flowing now very fast. It is so great and swift that there are those who will be afraid. They will try to hold on to the shore. They will feel they are being torn apart and will suffer greatly.

Know the river has its destination. The elders say we must let go of the shore, push off into the middle of the river, keep our eyes open, and our heads above the water. And I say, see who is in there with you and celebrate

....

The time of the lone wolf is over

....

We are the ones we've been waiting for.

THEME

CONNECTING WITH OTHER SOULS

The original source of these verses has been lost in time,[28] but British author Richard Barrett (1945–) often quotes the "Wisdom of the Elders" in his speeches and blogs. Barrett spent years as a consultant to and employee of the World Bank before starting his own firm, now known as the Barrett Values Centre. The author of numerous books (including *What My Soul Told Me* and *The New Leadership Paradigm*) based on his studies in psychology, spirituality, and physics, Barrett posits a higher level of consciousness where all souls are connected.

Barrett uses the ancient verses to encourage us to let go of our egos (the shore that we cling to) and trust the flow (in the river) of what our souls intend for us as they connect with the souls of everyone else. The river is the collection of souls moving inexorably to their ultimate destination.

In one of his blogs, Barrett writes,

Trusting your soul requires immense courage when you are operating as an ego. That is because the ego takes its job very seriously. It was given the task of keeping the body safe from harm, and it forgot that it was performing this service on behalf of the soul. It thought it was protecting itself. Your ego has to learn that to find true fulfillment it has to become the servant of your soul ... [People] are in the river with you for a reason. They are kindred souls; together you are going to shift into a state of interdependence so you can leverage your efforts in making a difference in the world.[29]

Barrett takes the view that we are all souls having a human experience. In his view, because all souls are connected at a higher level of consciousness, our true purpose is to connect with those other souls also having a human experience. Together, we make a difference in the world. That's Barrett's new paradigm of leadership. "The time of the lone wolf is over." "We are the ones we've been waiting for."

Or as various contemporary leaders have said, paraphrasing Hillel the Elder's words,

If not us, who? If not now, when?

PRACTICAL APPLICATIONS

1. Is your self-protecting ego making you cling to assumptions that separate you from other kindred souls?

2. Are you operating as a lone wolf?

3. Can you release yourself today from some of your ego barriers to connect at a soul-deep level with some kindred spirits?

Good leaders connect at a deep level with the souls of others.

SHALL I ALWAYS BE LEFT BEHIND?

J.R.R. TOLKIEN

[Eowyn] said bitterly. "Shall I always be left behind when the Riders depart, to mind the house while they win renown, and find food and beds when they return?"

...

"All your words are but to say: you are a woman, and your part is in the house. But when the men have died in battle and honour, you have leave to be burned in the house, for the men will need it no more. But I am of the House of Eorl and not a serving-woman. I can ride and wield blade, and I do not fear either pain or death."

"What do you fear, lady?" [Aragorn] asked.

"A cage," she said. "To stay behind bars, until use and old age accept them, and all chance of doing great deeds is gone beyond recall or desire."

THEME

LETTING LEADERS EMERGE

J.R.R. Tolkien (1892–1973) was a superb English writer and Oxford professor. He wrote *The Lord of the Rings* trilogy between 1937 and 1949. I remember finishing the first book, *The Fellowship of the Ring*, late one night and immediately picking up the second, *The Two Towers*. The trilogy is an epic, a high-fantasy saga about hobbits and their band of committed colleagues-wizards, elves, dwarfs, and more in Middle-Earth battling against the forces of evil: orcs, trolls, giant spiders, and dark lords.

Tolkien's masterful trilogy is rife with leadership lessons including fellowship, courage, commitment, persistence, and honor. The passage above from *The Return of the King*, focuses on the role of women.

Aragorn was a Ranger of the North, is proven to be the heir to the throne of Gondor, and is crowned King. Eowyn is the niece of King Theoden and longs to do great deeds in battle but is rejected because she is a woman. Undaunted, she disguises herself as a man and travels with the Riders of Rohan, ultimately confronting the evil Lord of the Nazgul, who boasts that he cannot fall "by the hand of man." Eowyn then removes her helmet, declaring, "But no living man am I! You look upon a woman" She then slays the Nazgul lord, thus turning the tide of the battle.

During my career, I had the wonderful pleasure of working with and promoting many extraordinary women: Ru Britton (corporate strategy); Deb Coller (corporate communications, who led a team that took on the FDA for its spurious allegations against our firm); Anne Pol (who ran the manufacturing plants at Pitney Bowes in Connecticut); Murem Sharpe (who successfully formed and led a new business); Wilemia Shaw and Susan Wallberg (two extraordinarily talented HR leaders); Alison Tanner (e-commerce and investor relations); and Denise Delaney, Jennifer Hayes, and Ellen Mitchell (on various boards of directors); just to name a few.

Then, of course, there were the extraordinary senior-executive women Gregg and I interviewed for *Triple Crown Leadership*: Ursula Burns (Xerox), Kit Crawford (Clif Bar), Elizabeth Crossman (Habitat for Humanity), Cheryl Dorsey (Echoing Green), Lynn Easterling (Cisco), Judy Gilbert (Google), Vanessa Kirsch (New Profit), Lorrie Norrington (eBay), Sharon Oster (Yale), Shirley Tilghman (Princeton), Mary Ann Tocio (Bright Horizons Family Solutions), and Nancy Tuor Moore (CH2M).

And of course I find within my own family circle remarkable women including my wife, June, my sister, Ann, and my daughters-in-law, Lori and Kristina, extraordinary all.

Like Eowyn, these women with heart, passion, and commitment are not content to be kept in cages.

PRACTICAL APPLICATIONS

1. What stereotypes still influence your leadership?
2. What might you do to loosen and discard some of these stereotypes?
3. Who could help you be more open-minded?

Good leaders will emerge from many places in your fellowship.

LITTLE BY LITTLE WEAN YOURSELF

RUMI

Little by little, wean yourself.
This is the gist of what I have to say.
From an embryo, whose nourishment comes in the blood,
move to an infant drinking milk,
to a child on solid food,
to a searcher after wisdom,
to a hunter of more invisible game.
Think how it is to have a conversation with an embryo.
You might say, "The world outside is vast and intricate.
There are wheatfields and mountain passes,
and orchards in bloom.
At night there are millions of galaxies, and in sunlight
the beauty of friends dancing at a wedding."
You ask the embryo why he, or she, stays cooped up
in the dark with eyes closed.

We must become ignorant
Of all we've been taught,
And be, instead bewildered.

Run from what's profitable and comfortable
If you drink those licquers, you'll spill
The spring water of your real life.

Forget safety.
Live where you fear to live.
Destroy your reputation.
Be notorious.

I have tried prudent planning
Long enough, from now
On, I'll live mad.

THEME

TAKING CHANCES

Jalal ad-Din Muhammad Rumi (1207–1273) was a Persian poet, scholar, and Sufi mystic, whose works are widely read today. In "Little by Little Wean Yourself," Rumi speaks of the constant need to move beyond the comfort of our own safety zones and into the vast and terrifying unknown. The embryo must leave the womb to become an infant, before progressing to become a child, then a searcher for wisdom, and then a hunter of "more invisible game," perhaps a metaphor for the search for meaning in life, what one's true purpose is, or what one's soul truly hungers for?

Rumi says the embryo stage, being safe within the womb, is our comfort zone. In the process of weaning ourselves, we become ignorant again, giving up the mastery we enjoyed where we were secure. That security is what makes change so difficult. We must "run from what's profitable and comfortable," otherwise we'll "spill the spring water" of our lives. We must forget "safety" and "prudent planning" and live "notorious" and "mad" instead. It's not easy to step down that way, out of our comfort zones, but it's essential if we are to step up to the potential of what we might be.

In my search to find a "better way to lead," I worked over the course of thirty years in many different industries from low-tech to high-tech. It was daunting to break into new industries, but it stretched my mind, challenged my assumptions, and made me dig deeper to find what we, together, could do to resurrect the business. In *every* case, I found wonderful colleagues willing and patient to teach me what I didn't know and what they each had to offer. I remember getting regular technology tutorials from the Chief Technology Officer and his staff at one major high-tech firm where I was CEO. I willingly admitted to them how much I didn't know about what they already took for granted. It was humbling but essential.

I became a better leader and a better person by being willing to venture forth from the known into the unknown. Ultimately, my fear of change dissipated, and I *knew* we, together, could enter any void and find our way through.

PRACTICAL APPLICATIONS

1. Are you stuck in a comfort zone?
2. Are you fearful of venturing forth because you don't know what you'll encounter?
3. What might you do today, little by little, to wean yourself toward the spring water of your real life?

Leading well and living well mean taking chances to venture forth.

THE CHARGE OF THE LIGHT BRIGADE

ALFRED LORD TENNYSON

Half a league, half a league,
Half a league onward,
All in the valley of Death
Rode the six hundred.
"Forward, the Light Brigade!
Charge for the guns!" he said.
Into the valley of Death
Rode the six hundred.

"Forward, the Light Brigade!"
Was there a man dismayed?
Not though the soldier knew
Someone had blundered.
Theirs not to make reply,
Theirs not to reason why,
Theirs but to do and die.
Into the valley of Death
Rode the six hundred.

Cannon to right of them,
Cannon to left of them,
Cannon in front of them
Volleyed and thundered;
Stormed at with shot and shell,
Boldly they rode and well,
Into the jaws of Death,
Into the mouth of hell
Rode the six hundred.

...

THEME

CARING FOR YOUR FOLLOWERS

Alfred Lord Tennyson (1809–1892) was Britain's Poet Laureate during much of Queen Victoria's reign. His poem, "The Charge of the Light Brigade," describes the British Light Cavalry charge at the battle of Balaclava during the Crimean War in 1854. It recounts a disastrous frontal assault against an embedded artillery battery due to miscommunication in the chain of command.[30] Many readers of this infamous charge focus on the bravery, loyalty, and discipline of the British Light Cavalry in riding into certain death. Those traits are admirable, indeed, although some might say foolhardy in this particular battle.

My focus, though, is on the "blunder." Historians dispute what exactly happened in this tragic charge, but it is clear that a mistake was made when orders were passed, or interpreted, for the brigade to charge into a valley protected on all sides by cannons. It was certain suicide, and the brigade was massacred.

As leaders, we have a solemn responsibility for the people who rely on us, trust us, and follow our directives, sometimes even without question. Early in my career, too often I expected people to work the same hours I did and to sacrifice heroically for our business objectives. That was wrong of me. I wasn't thinking about them and their families, or caring for them personally.

As we make leadership decisions, we must ensure, to the best of our ability, that we are not sending our people into Tennyson's "mouth of hell." As former U.S. president Theodore Roosevelt once said,

People don't care how much you know until they know how much you care.

PRACTICAL APPLICATIONS

1. Do you carefully consider the effect of your decisions on your people?
2. Are you burning them out?
3. Are you caring for their well-being?
4. What might you do, starting today, to care better for those you lead?

Leading well means caring for the well-being of those you lead.

MORALITY ABOVE 8,000 METERS

JON KRAKAUER

... two Japanese climbers, accompanied by three Sherpas, set out for the [Everest] summit from the same high camp on the Northeast Ridge that the Ladakhis [a region in India and Pakistan on the border of China] had used ... At 6:00 A.M. ... [they] were taken aback to see one of the Ladakhi climbers ... lying in the snow, horribly frostbitten but still alive after a night without shelter or oxygen, moaning unintelligibly. Not wanting to jeopardize their ascent by stopping to assist him, the Japanese team continued climbing toward the summit.

...

Just beyond the top of the Second Step they came upon the other two Ladakhis

...

According to an article in the *Financial Times* ... one of the Ladakhis was "apparently close to death, the other crouching in the snow. No words were passed. No water, food or oxygen exchanged hands. The Japanese moved on and 160 feet farther along they rested and exchanged oxygen cylinders."

...

"We didn't know them. No, we didn't give them any water. We didn't talk to them. They had severe high-altitude sickness. They looked as if they were dangerous."

...

"We were too tired to help. Above 8,000 meters is not a place where people can afford morality."

THEME

MORALITY UNDER DURESS

Jon Krakauer (1954–) is an American writer and mountaineer. He is the author of best-selling books including *Into Thin Air*, which recounts the 1996 expedition to summit Mount Everest, during which eight climbers were killed, including world-class guides, clients, and Sherpas. Everest is the highest mountain on Earth at 8,848 meters (29,029 feet) above sea level.

Summiting Everest has long been an obsession for many in spite of the extreme hardships, including the risk of death, extreme cold and gale-high winds, avalanches, altitude sickness that can cause delirium, and more. To summit Everest, one must marshal an extreme desire to succeed, money to pay the enormous costs, have experience in mountaineering, and months of training and acclimatization. To summit Everest, one needs to be almost compulsively fanatical. Taken too far, this commitment becomes what's known as summit fever.

Veteran mountain climbers can understand why the Japanese climbers, suffering from their own decreased mental faculties, decided to not render aid to fellow climbers who were highly likely to die. Yet one of the American clients on another part of the 1996 expedition was twice given up for dead but survived, albeit with extreme frostbite that ultimately necessitated the amputation of his right hand.

In contrast there were many other climbers and guides on this same expedition who, without hesitation, sacrificed their own attempts to summit Everest, giving their oxygen, medical supplies, and aid to rescue others. Their ethical values, even at 8,000 meters, were greater than their obsession to reach the summit.

Some people have obsessive goals and surrender their ethical compass in their pursuit. Lance Armstrong was so obsessed with winning the Tour de France bicycle races that he devised and concealed a protracted doping regimen that he got away with for years. Others, like polar explorer Ernest Shackleton, go to extraordinary and heroic measures to safeguard their colleagues. Some organizations set an obsessive, superordinate goals, such as Enron did; or such as Toyota, GM, and VW did in their quest to gain market share and be number one.

PRACTICAL APPLICATIONS

1. Would you be able to live with yourself if you sacrificed your ethical principles to achieve your summit fever?
2. Before you face a crisis, before your mind is clouded with your obsessive goal, decide what ethical principles are inviolable.

Good leaders have an intense desire to succeed but not at the expense of their ethical values.

A RETURN TO LOVE

MARIANNE WILLIAMSON

Our deepest fear is not that we are inadequate.

Our deepest fear is that we are powerful beyond measure.

It is our light, not our darkness, that most frightens us.

We ask ourselves, who am I to be brilliant, gorgeous, talented and fabulous?

Actually, who are you not to be?

You are a child of God.

Your playing small does not serve the world.

There is nothing enlightened about shrinking so that other people

Will not feel insecure around you.

We were born to make and manifest the glory of God that is within us.

It is not just in some of us; it is in everyone.

And as we let our own light shine,

We unconsciously give other people permission to do the same.

As we are liberated from our own fear,

Our presence automatically liberates others.

THEME

LETTING YOUR LIGHT SHINE

"A Return to Love" is commonly attributed to Nelson Mandela's 1994 inaugural speech, but Marianne Williamson wrote these words in her 1992 book, *A Return to Love,* based on her reading of *A Course in Miracles.*[31] Williamson (1952–) is an American best-selling author and speaker. Her message resonates deeply with my own experience.

So many people wallow as victims. They disempower themselves by saying, "Who am I to stand up, raise my voice, or take the lead. I'm just a _____." Then fill in the blank, "I'm just a housewife. I'm just a clerk. I'm just an engineer, or a truck driver."

Williamson's words remind me of the brown-bag lunch we had at a company where I was CEO. Volunteers from different departments would sign-up to join me for lunch. We'd sit in a conference room and go around the table, introducing ourselves, asking and answering questions, and then always discussing some challenge that the department faced. At one of these lunches, we were discussing an engineering challenge, and I had a brilliant idea. I couldn't wait until my turn to speak. Perhaps I could show how worthy I was of being their CEO? Then a young engineer, let's call her Kathy, spoke "my" idea.

What should I do? Should I say, "I was thinking the same thing" and then launch into my details of the idea? Fortunately, I stifled my thoughts and asked her to elaborate. Then I asked her to sketch out the solution on the whiteboard. Then I asked if she'd like to head-up a cross-functional, special-action team to implement the idea. She said, "Me? Oh, no. I'm *just* an engineer."

Everyone present agreed that Kathy could and should lead that team. She left that brown-bag lunch with a special assignment to lead a cross-functional team. The team was wildly successful, and Kathy was subsequently promoted. Soon, many people wanted to lead a special-action team. They were leaders unleashed.

My experience is that everyone has hidden gifts. Everyone can lead, just for a brief time if they wish, and if they make that choice. Anyone can stand up, be heard, or offer a voice. But too many don't. Perhaps beaten down by parents, teachers, bosses, peers, and especially by their own insecurities?

PRACTICAL APPLICATIONS

1. Are you disempowering yourself with negative thoughts?
2. What three things might you do today to lift this negative mindset?
3. What special talents do you have that you might share with the world?

Living and leading well mean letting your own inner light shine through.

DEALING WITH A DEAD HORSE
(MY REPHRASING OF EXCERPTS)

AUTHOR UNKNOWN

How does a bureaucratic organization deal with a dead horse?

1. Change the rider.
2. Buy a stronger whip.
3. Beat the horse harder.
4. Shout at the horse.
5. Appoint a committee to study the horse.
6. Visit other places to see how they ride dead horses.
7. Increase the standards for riding dead horses.
8. Appoint a committee to revive the dead horse.
9. Create a training session to improve riding skills.
10. Explore the state of dead horses in today's environment.
11. Change the requirements so that the horse no longer meets the standards of death.
12. Hire a consultant to show how to ride a dead horse.
13. Harness several dead horses together to increase speed.
14. Increase funding to improve the horse's performance.
15. Declare that no horse is too dead to ride.
16. Fund a study to determine if outsourcing will reduce the cost of riding a dead horse.
17. Buy a computer program to enhance the dead horse's performance.
18. Declare a dead horse less costly to maintain than a live one.
19. Form a work group to find uses for dead horses.

And if all else fails:

20. Promote the dead horse to a supervisory position.

THEME

DEALING WITH REALITY

Many versions of "Dealing with a Dead Horse" can be found in circulation. I was unable to confirm the original version and author, so I've rephrased some excerpts in my own words. These curious verses appeal to me in a perverse way because, like Dilbert cartoons, they hit close to home with their insightful but sarcastic and ironic truth.

I have to admit that in my leadership career I often found myself riding some dead horses. I changed the rider, beat the horse harder, appointed committees, hired consultants, threw more money at the horse, and more. What a waste.

Sometimes we live in denial. Sometimes we have so much money or effort invested in a project, we can't let go. That money and time is a sunk cost. What really matters is the future money and effort necessary to reach success in comparison to the alternatives where that money and effort could be spent.

What often keeps us beating a dead horse is that the project is our own pet idea, and we have our own egos invested in its success. We fear admitting failure. We fear the embarrassment before our peers and superiors. So, we keep beating that dead horse. When you are riding a dead horse, instead of refusing to quit, you need to get off and find a different steed.

Good leaders face reality. They can perceive if the horse they are riding is still alive with a chance to succeed, or if the horse is dead. They don't engage in elaborate Kabuki dances to pretend otherwise. Maybe they hold a ceremony to celebrate the life and death of their noble horse. They may choose to learn why this horse died so they don't kill any others. But they don't stay in denial with bureaucratic excuses that don't reflect reality. They courageously admit a mistake, take time to learn from it, spread those lessons to others, and bravely ride on.

PRACTICAL APPLICATIONS

1. Are you riding any dead horses at work, or in your personal life?
2. Have you been engaging in elaborate charades in the hope your horse will arise from the dead?
3. What new horse can you mount starting today?

Good leaders acknowledge reality, dismount dead horses, and ride mounts that will get them where they want to go.

SWING

DAVID HALBERSTAM

When most oarsmen talked about their perfect moments in a boat, they referred not so much to winning a race, as to the feel of the boat, all eight oars in the water together, the synchronization almost perfect. In moments like these, the boat seemed to lift right out of the water. Oarsmen called that the moment of swing.

THEME

ACHIEVING FLOW

David Halberstam (1934–2007) was a Pulitzer Prize winning journalist, historian, and author. His book *The Amateurs* published in 1985 recounts the story of four young men on their quest to win an Olympic medal in the sport of crew or rowing. I love this passage about oarsmen reaching the moment of "swing" and often quote it in my leadership workshops because I get goose bumps when I recite it.

"Swing" is most commonly known as "flow" or "being in the zone," a mental state "in which a person performing an activity is fully immersed in a feeling of energized focus, full involvement, and enjoyment in the process of the activity."[32] Mihaly Csikszentmihalyi, a Hungarian Professor of Psychology, has written about flow extensively. Most people think flow applies only to sports teams, but I have been blessed to experience it in the workplace. After my first flow/swing experience, described below, everything changed for me.

In 1981, when I was president of Monarch Marking Systems, we commissioned a cross-functional team of volunteers to launch a breakthrough product in half the normal time. We located the team in special quarters off-site, and (based on some wise coaching by a talented VP of R&D, Bud Klein) I delegated to the team *all* my authority as president, as long as they operated by our shared values and met some explicit goals in a clear priority order. It was the biggest challenge of their careers, and I took a lot of heat from our corporate parent because we weren't authorized to launch such a project without corporate's approval.

Eighteen months later (and, indeed, in half the normal development time), under the leadership of a talented, young engineering leader, Jim Vanderpool, the committed and empowered team successfully launched the breakthrough product, setting the industry standard. Afterward, no one on the team wanted to return to their old ways of working in engineering, purchasing, or marketing. They had achieved a new state of flow in their work. For them, that flow experience was a game changer.

So, we literally reinvented that company, deploying such radically empowered teams everywhere that we possibly could. The results were spectacular, and the people in the organization soared.

PRACTICAL APPLICATIONS

1. Do you trust teams to achieve incredible results by radically empowering them?
2. Can you launch an empowered team today on a special project to see if they can achieve flow?

Good leaders radically empower people to achieve an incredible state of flow.

O CAPTAIN! MY CAPTAIN!

WALT WHITMAN

O Captain! My Captain! Our fearful trip is done,

The ship has weather's every rack, the prize we sought is won,

The port is near, the bells I hear, the people all exulting,

While follow eyes the steady keel, the vessel grim and daring;

But O heart! Heart! Heart!

O the bleeding drops of red,

Where on the deck my Captain lies,

Fallen cold and dead.

O Captain! My Captain! Rise up and hear the bells;

Rise up-for you the flag is flung-for you the bugle trills,

For you bouquets and ribbon's wreaths-for you the shores a-crowding,

For you they call, the swaying mass, their eager faces turning;

Here Captain! Dear father!

This arm beneath your head!

It is some dream that on the deck,

You've fallen cold and dead.

My Captain does not answer, his lips are pale and still,

My father does not feel my arm, he has no pulse nor will,

The ship is anchor'd safe and sound, its voyage closed and done,

From fearful trip the victor ship comes in with object won;

Exult O shores, and ring O bells!

But I with mournful tread,

Walk the deck my Captain lies,

Fallen cold and dead.

THEME

HONORING YOUR LEADERS

Walt Whitman (1819–1892) was one of America's most influential poets and is often called the father of free verse. He wrote "O Captain! My Captain!" after the assassination of Abraham Lincoln in 1865.

During Lincoln's tenure as president, he bore grave burdens. He lost a son to illness, suffered from depression, was maligned by many, and made difficult decisions to keep the states in a Union. Today, some experts consider Lincoln to be the greatest of our presidents. Yet, Lincoln did not have the benefit of such support when he was alive.

Too often, we don't express our appreciation to the leaders, influencers, and formal or informal mentors in our lives who have guided us. Then suddenly, it's too late. They are gone to another assignment after they have brought their ships to safe harbors, or worse like Lincoln, are lying "fallen, cold and dead."

I wish now I could have in-person conversations again with my father, my mother, again with Robert Greenleaf and Jan Erteszek, and others. I didn't realize it at the time that they were making a huge impression on my life. I thank them now in my prayers, but I wish I had acknowledged them better when I was in their presence. I wish I had told them how much their counsel meant to me. I now occasionally reach out to people I have worked for, or with, or have met who have influenced me. It's just a phone call, or a short visit, but I think and hope they appreciate my reaching out to them.

I reached out recently to Tom Loemker, a former Pitney Bowes executive who hired me to be president of Monarch Marking Systems and later asked me to join him at Pitney Bowes' HQ. Tom was the best boss I ever had, supportive, encouraging, and gave me the freedom to blaze new paths, even highly unconventional ones. I knew Tom had my back, cared about me personally, and trusted my judgment. Working for Tom was a joy. It was important for me to tell Tom how I felt about his leadership.

PRACTICAL APPLICATIONS

1. Who are the influential captains in your life who have guided you and borne burdens on your behalf?

2. Have you told them what they have meant to you?

3. Starting today, contact these influencers to express your appreciation to them. I think you'll be pleased, and so will they.

Leading well involves honoring the influencers who have guided you.

PART III

LEAVING A LEADERSHIP LEGACY

"The leader's unique legacy is the creation of valued institutions that survive over time."

—Jim Kouzes and Barry Posner, leadership experts
and best-selling authors

ood leadership has many dimensions. One of the more overlooked dimensions is the legacy a leader leaves. When Gregg and I wrote *Triple Crown Leadership,* we cited the three E's of great leadership: building an *excellent,* *ethical,* and *enduring* organization. The enduring element touches on the legacy that great leadership leaves.

If a leader accomplishes great achievements with his or her organization, but then everything falls apart when the leader is gone, there has been no long-lasting and positive change that made the world better. Good leadership leaves a legacy that carries on, is appreciated, and long remembered.

A leadership legacy has many dimensions that answer these questions:

1. What has been built into the DNA of the organization that will carry on?
    a. Is there a meaningful shared purpose the organization has embraced?
    b. Are shared values inculcated into the organization to guide proper behaviors?
    c. Is there an exciting and inspiring vision of the future?
    d. Is there a healthy, vibrant culture? Culture is the legacy of leadership.

2. How was success achieved?
    a. Were corners cut?
    b. Was integrity absent?
    c. Were any stakeholders abused?
    d. Was the long-term continually sacrificed for the short-term?
    e. Was the leader a good role model?
        i.   Did he or she value people and treat them respectfully?
        ii. Did he or she help others grow and develop?

3. What is the quality of the people at all levels who remain?
    a. Are they people with character, showing heart?
    b. Are they properly skilled?

    c. Are they growing other leaders?

    d. Are they passionate about the purpose of the organization, willing to fight for what's right?

    e. Do they respect and trust each other, working collaboratively to unleash their creativity?

4. Do stories about the organization's past inform its present?

    a. Are these stories often told to provide guidance when new challenges are being faced?

    b. Are these stories about the heroics of the departed leader (not so good), or how the departed leader helped others be heroic (much better)?

We can find answers to these questions in the words of wisdom that poets and writers have shared with us over the years.

JABBERWOCKY

LEWIS CARROLL

`Twas brillig, and the slithy toves
Did gyre and gimble in the wabe:
All mimsy were the borogoves,
And the mome raths outgrabe.

"Beware the Jabberwock, my son!
The jaws that bite, the claws that catch!
Beware the Jubjub bird, and shun
The frumious Bandersnatch!"
He took his vorpal sword in hand:
Long time the manxome foe he sought-
So rested he by the Tumtum tree,
And stood awhile in thought.
And, as in uffish thought he stood,
The Jabberwock, with eyes of flame,
Came whiffling through the tulgey wood,
And burbled as it came!
One, two! One, two! And through and through
The vorpal blade went snicker-snack!
He left it dead, and with its head
He went galumphing back.
"And, has thou slain the Jabberwock?
Come to my arms, my beamish boy!
O frabjous day! Callooh! Callay!"
He chortled in his joy.

`Twas brillig, and the slithy toves
Did gyre and gimble in the wabe;
All mimsy were the borogoves,
And the mome raths outgrabe.

THEME

EMBARKING ON THE QUEST

Lewis Carroll (1832–1898) was an English writer, logician, and Anglican deacon noted for his skills with curious verse and fantasy writing. He was the author of *Alice's Adventures in Wonderland*. "Jabberwocky" is from his 1871 novel *Through the Looking-Glass and What Alice Found There*. I have recited it often to family and friends over the years.

The poem "Jabberwocky" appears in a book Alice is reading, and she asks Humpty-Dumpty to help her understand the strange, nonsensical words she encounters. He explains, for example, that "brillig means 4 o'clock in the afternoon-the time when you begin broiling things for dinner."

To me, besides its enjoyable and whimsical verse, "Jabberwocky" tells the timeless story of the quest in which the hero ventures out into the unknown to slay the beasts that threaten and then returns galumphing in triumph. (According to Humpty-Dumpty, galumphing is a combination of "gallop" and "triumph").

An intriguing part of the poem to me is in the opening stanza repeated at the closing. I interpret the repeated stanza to mean there will always be new quests for leaders to undertake. No matter our past heroics in slaying the Jabberwocks out there in the world, other monsters remain to confront. The leader must venture out again and again. Someone must bravely lead and take up the causes because each of us can accomplish fabulous feats, slaying the terrible dragons in the world.

I agree with author Max DePree, who once wrote,

Leadership is a quest.

PRACTICAL APPLICATIONS

1. What is the noble quest you should undertake?
2. What's keeping you from taking up your vorpal sword and seeking out the manxome foe?

Good leaders pursue noble quests.

WHAT CONSTITUTES SUCCESS

BESSIE STANLEY

He has achieved success who has lived well,

Laughed often and loved much

Who has gained the respect of intelligent men

And the love of little children

Who has filled his niche and accomplished his task

Who has left the world better than he found it

Whether by an improved poppy, a perfect poem, or a rescued soul

Who has never lacked appreciation of earth's beauty or failed to express it

Who has always looked for the best in others and given them the best he had

Whose life was an inspiration

Whose memory a benediction.

THEME

DEFINING SUCCESS

American poet Elisabeth-Anne ("Bessie") Anderson Stanley (1879–1952) wrote "What Constitutes Success" in 1904. A version of it is inaccurately attributed to Ralph Waldo Emerson and to Robert Louis Stevenson.

How we define success makes all the difference in our lives. Some set out on the path to fame and fortune, or seeking recognition and praise, comparing themselves constantly to others, and invariably coming up short since there will always be others who have achieved more.

Bessie Stanley captures a better definition of success: laughing often, loving much, gaining respect and the love of children, accomplishing tasks, appreciating beauty and nature, and giving the best you can so that your life is an inspiration to others. These are noble goals, indeed, and we have heard them in the words of other poets.

Most of all, though, as I have come to think about it, success is about leaving the world a little bit better than you found it. My original goals in life revolved around how much money I would earn and how expensive a house we might be able to afford someday. Then I transitioned to a goal of wanting to "run something," anything, as long as I was running it.

It took me years to realize that the true purpose of my life, how success would ultimately be defined for me, was simply to leave the world a little better place through the character of our children and grandchildren, through the organizations where I worked, and through what I could contribute to the leadership literature. That's the benediction I finally hope to earn as a son, husband, father, grandfather, brother, lifelong student of leadership, and trusted colleague.

PRACTICAL APPLICATIONS

1. Make a list of how you have been defining success up until now.
2. Compare it to Stanley's list above.
3. Is your definition of success all about material goods or accomplishments?
4. Is your life truly an inspiration to others?
5. Beginning today, what alterations can you make to your success list?

Leading well and living a good life mean being wise in how you define success.

OZYMANDIAS

PERCY BYSSHE SHELLEY

I met a traveler from an antique land
Who said: "Two vast and trunkless legs of stone
Stand in the desert

. . .

Near them, on the sand,
Half sunk, a shattered visage lies, whose frown,
And wrinkled lip, and sneer of cold command,
Tell that its sculptor well those passions read,
Which yet survive, stamped on these lifeless things,
The hand that mocked them, and the heart that fed:
And on the pedestal these words appear:
'My name is Ozymandias, king of kings:
Look on my works, ye Mighty, and despair!'
Nothing beside remains. Round the decay
Of that colossal wreck, boundless and bare
The lone and level sands stretch far away."

THEME

LEAVING A LEGACY OF HUBRIS

Percy Bysshe Shelley (1792–1822) was an English romantic, lyric, and epic poet who published "Ozymandias" in 1818. Ozymandias is the Greek name for the Egyptian pharaoh, Ramesses II (1303–1213 BCE), often regarded as the greatest pharaoh of the Egyptian Empire.

In Shelley's poem, we see the broken head of a statue depicting a sneering, cold, commanding leader, a king of kings, who feels even the mighty will despair when they gaze upon his wondrous works. But surrounding this shattered visage is boundless, bare, and bleak desert.

Our own presumed greatness becomes hubris, a word from the ancient Greeks that means excessive pride or overconfidence that offends the gods. In Greek mythology, hubris is a common theme, illustrated, for example, by the fall of Icarus, who flies with wings constructed of feathers and wax. He ignores his father's warning not to fly too high. The sun melts the wax, and Icarus plunges to his death in the sea. An antonym for hubris is humility, which (along with the will to succeed) celebrated leadership author, Jim Collins, cites in his best-selling book *Good to Great* as an essential quality for his "Level V" leader.

I remember with embarrassment parking my convertible sports car in the fire lane at the corporate HQ of one company where I worked as a Group VP while I went upstairs to attend a meeting. I didn't want to bother going into the corporate lot to find a parking space. People who recognized my car must have considered me an arrogant jerk. Who did I think I was?

Shelley's poem reveals how people assess and depict us for posterity. People don't remember Ozymandias for the great buildings, temples, and cities he had his slaves build, or the wars that he won. They remember his sneering arrogance, pretension, and the conceit that the sculptors captured in his visage.

People will remember how you treated other people, especially them. If your treatment is respectful, fair, and honorable, you may, indeed, have monuments to your memory that will be better than Ozymandias' "colossal wreck."

PRACTICAL APPLICATIONS

1. How do people view you today?
2. Are you cold, commanding, arrogant, or cynical?
3. Do the trappings that surround you consume you?
4. How will you be remembered?
5. What might you do starting today to improve how you'll be remembered?

Humility, not hubris, is essential in good leadership.

FEW WILL HAVE THE GREATNESS

ROBERT F. KENNEDY

Few will have the greatness to bend history; but each of us can work to change a small portion of events, and in the total of all those acts will be written the history of this generation

...

It is from numberless diverse acts of courage and belief that human history is thus shaped. Each time a man stands up for an ideal, or acts to improve the lot of others, or strikes out against injustice, he sends forth a tiny ripple of hope, and crossing each other from a million different centers of energy and daring, those ripples build a current which can sweep down the mightiest walls of oppression and resistance.

THEME

MAKING RIPPLES

Attorney General of the U.S. Robert F. Kennedy (1925–1968) spoke these powerful words in June 1966 during a visit to South Africa. At the time, that country was going through an agonizing period of unrest concerning racial segregation. Nelson Mandela and other anti-apartheid activists were jailed on Robben Island. Kennedy's words became known as the "Ripple of Hope Speech." It was hailed as one of the most significant speeches of the twentieth century. On that same South African trip, Robert Kennedy, paraphrasing a biblical passage, also said,

Who will sound the trumpet? And to what battle are we called?

Few of us will bend history, but each of us can make some ripples. Others will notice, and some will be inspired to make their own ripples. Thus, collectively, we do bend history. The 14th Dalai Lama said,

Just as ripples spread out when a single pebble is dropped into water,
the actions of individuals can have far-reaching effects.

I learned over the years to make ripples in organizations that were stuck in outmoded leadership models. I sat on the other side of the table, alongside the union reps, facing my management colleagues to show that we were really all working for the same organization. I periodically worked in the factories in jeans to earn workers' trust. I ignored bureaucratic corporate policies to produce better results faster. I purchased computers without corporate approval to empower our managers. I shared our confidential financials with key vendors to find collaborative ways to cut our costs together (a highly successful tactic). I often took heat for my unconventional actions, but I have no regrets about sounding some trumpets and making some ripples, many of which generated useful waves of change.

In their own small way, my ripples made an impression on people around me, helping them find their own strong leadership voices, encouraging them to challenge wrongs and make them right, inspiring them to think more deeply about their own life purpose or our organizational purpose, and role modeling for them a better brand of leadership.

PRACTICAL APPLICATIONS

1. What's the issue that burns inside you asking to be addressed?
2. Can you make a list of a few ripples you can make today, or trumpets you will sound, on that issue?
3. Then ask some others you trust what your ripples meant to them.
4. Maybe together you'll start a current flowing?

Leading well means making ripples.

HIS EXAMPLE

EDGAR GUEST

There are little eyes upon you, and they're watching night and day;
There are little ears that quickly take in every word you say;
There are little hands all eager to do everything you do,
And a little boy that's dreaming of the day he'll be like you.

You're the little fellow's idol, you're the wisest of the wise;
In his little mind about you no suspicions ever rise;
He believes in you devoutly, holds that all you say and do
He will say and do in your way when he's grown up just like you.

Oh, it sometimes makes me shudder when I hear my boy repeat
Some careless phrase I've uttered in the language of the street;
And it sets my heart to grieving when some little fault I see
And I know beyond all doubting that he picked it up from me.

There's a wide-eyed little fellow who believes you're always right,
And his ears are always open and he watches day and night;
You are setting an example every day in all you do
For the little boy who's waiting to grow up to be like you.

THEME

BEING A ROLE MODEL

Edgar Guest (1881–1959), whom we visited with his poem "Don't Quit," was a popular American writer. Guest's poem "His Example" was published in his book *The Path to Home* in 1919. Guest's powerful message applies to all of us.

Our attitudes and actions set an example for many: our colleagues, peers, friends, spouses, and, especially, our sons and daughters whose little eyes and ears are constantly open to what we are doing. They observe whether our actions are consistent with our words. Are we walking our talk?

I wish I could look back on my parenting and know I was an exemplary father, but I can't. I was too absent, too focused on career, too reliant on my dear wife to provide the parenting our sons needed (and, fortunately, got from her).

I wish I could look back on my business career and know I was an exemplary role model for the behavior I espoused, but I can't. At times, I was too intense and impatient, too worried and demanding, too pressuring and intimidating.

I'm human, of course, but that doesn't excuse my bad behavior. I realized slowly that I needed to strive to be better, to be a role model for others. And when I mess up, as I invariably do, then I need to sincerely apologize and try my very best not to make that same mistake again.

PRACTICAL APPLICATIONS

1. Are you short tempered with people?
2. Are you impatient and upset when others don't do what you want them to do?
3. Are you controlling towards others?
4. Are you being the exemplary role model you should be for the children around you?
5. Make a list today of how you can be more patient with the faults of others, guiding them more gently.

Leading well means being an exemplary role model.

THE PARADOXICAL COMMANDMENTS

DR. KENT M. KEITH

People are illogical, unreasonable, and self-centered.
Love them anyway.

If you do good, people will accuse you of selfish ulterior motives.
Do good anyway.

If you are successful, you will win false friends and true enemies.
Succeed anyway.

The good you do today will be forgotten tomorrow.
Do good anyway.

Honesty and frankness make you vulnerable.
Be honest and frank anyway.

The biggest men and women with the biggest ideas can be shot down by the smallest men and women with the smallest minds.
Think big anyway.

People favor underdogs but follow only top dogs.
Fight for a few underdogs anyway.

What you spend years building may be destroyed overnight.
Build anyway.

People really need help but may attack you if you do help them.
Help people anyway.

Give the world the best you have and you'll get kicked in the teeth.
Give the world the best you have anyway.

THEME

DOING GOOD ANYWAY

Dr. Kent M. Keith (1948–) has had a distinguished career as a writer and leader in higher education and is currently the president of Pacific Rim Christian University in Hawaii. He wrote this poem in 1968 as part of a booklet for student leaders at age 19 when he was a student at Harvard. The poem has touched millions of people and is often called "Anyway." A version of it hung in Mother Teresa's home for children in Calcutta.

The lesson to be drawn here is that critics will always be present, finding fault, questioning your intentions, or jealous of your success. Your work will not always be appreciated, and it may be forgotten. Cynics and false friends, caught in their own negative mindsets, will snipe at what you attempt to do. As a leader, you will be attacked.

But all that doesn't matter. Letting others wrest control by assessing the worth of your work is wrong. You know your motives and what you have worked on building. Be resolute in your noble work regardless of the stings. They don't last long and will be forgotten when you succeed. So go forth undaunted. As Mahatma Gandhi once said,

First they ignore you, then they laugh at you, then they fight you, then you win.

My work trying to resurrect troubled companies or organizations that had huge challenges frequently came under heavy criticism. Sometimes all the possible options we faced had bad consequences. Yet, we had to choose and move forward, making many mid-course corrections along the way, and drawing much criticism in the process. I learned that the criticism comes with the territory of leadership, and I couldn't let it get me down-at least not for long. I knew our hearts were in the right place, our intentions were honorable, and that we had to keep moving forward *anyway*.

I also learned to listen to the critics instead of ignoring them. Often I gleaned something from what they said that would take us down a better path. Their message delivery or motives may have been poor, but there was often a kernel of truth in an attack. An old adage says,

Your management of an attack, more than the substance of the accusation, determines your fate.

PRACTICAL APPLICATIONS

1. Do you become discouraged when others denigrate your contributions?
2. Do you let other people define your self-worth?
3. If so, resolve today to do your best work with the noblest intentions regardless of the critics.
4. Just do it anyway.

Leading well means listening to your conscience and just doing good anyway.

GETTYSBURG ADDRESS

ABRAHAM LINCOLN

Four score and seven years ago our fathers brought forth on this continent, a new nation, conceived in Liberty, and dedicated to the proposition that all men are created equal.

Now we are engaged in a great civil war, testing whether that nation, or any nation so conceived and so dedicated, can long endure. We are met on a great battlefield of that war. We have come to dedicate a portion of that field, as a final resting place for those who here gave their lives that that nation might live. It is altogether fitting and proper that we should do this.

But, in a larger sense, we cannot dedicate-we cannot consecrate-we cannot hallow-this ground. The brave men, living and dead, who struggled here, have consecrated it, far above our poor power to add or detract. The world will little note, nor long remember what we say here, but it can never forget what they did here. It is for us the living, rather, to be dedicated here to the unfinished work, which they who fought here have thus far so nobly advanced. It is rather for us to be here dedicated to the great task remaining before us-that from these honored dead we take increased devotion to that cause for which they gave the last full measure of devotion-that we here highly resolve that these dead shall not have died in vain-that this nation, under God, shall have a new birth of freedom-and that government of the people, by the people, for the people, shall not perish from the earth.

THEME

HONORING YOUR PREDECESSORS

U. S. President Abraham Lincoln(1809–1865) delivered the Gettysburg Address on November 19, 1863 at the dedication of the Soldiers' National Cemetery in Gettysburg, Pennsylvania. The Battle of Gettysburg incurred the largest number of casualties on both sides of the Civil War (between 46,000 and 51,000) and is considered by some to have been a turning point for the Union.[33]

Lincoln's speech took just over two minutes to deliver but has reverberated over time as one the greatest in United States history. The noted orator, U.S. senator, governor, and Harvard president, Edward Everett, preceded Lincoln. His speech of over 13,000 words took over two hours to deliver and has been largely forgotten. Brevity trumps verbosity.

The prime focus of Lincoln's speech was to honor the dead at Gettysburg, but he sagely cast his words in the context of a unique nation brought forth by our "fathers" in the prior century. Of course, that nation was imperfect with its implicit sanction of slavery (which some of the Founders felt would die out over time) and which later led to this awful Civil War. Lincoln pays tribute to the Founding Fathers, imperfect as they were, and then depicts a new nation that these honored dead have helped to create where all men will truly be "equal."

In my experience, poor leaders often denigrate the work of the leaders who preceded them. Sometimes those leaders were terrible, and their work should be disparaged. But often, prior leaders did laudable work, even amid the errors they made. People will be confused if you completely disparage your predecessors because at times your followers likely resonated with their prior leaders and followed them willingly.

Lincoln didn't fault the Founders for the slavery they sanctioned. He honored the good contributions of the Founders and then forged ahead, building what morally needed to be built: a new freedom for people within the nation that would truly honor those who gave their lives at Gettysburg.

PRACTICAL APPLICATIONS

1. Are you honoring the good of those who preceded you?
2. Or are you criticizing and dumping all they did so you can start completely fresh?
3. How might you honor the positive contributions of those who preceded you, building on their accomplishments today?

Good leaders acknowledge and carry on the best of their predecessors.

SONNET 18

WILLIAM SHAKESPEARE

Shall I compare thee to a summer's day?

Thou art more lovely and more temperate:

Rough winds do shake the darling buds of May,

And summer's lease hath all too short a date;

Sometime too hot the eye of heaven shines,

And often is his gold complexion dimm'd;

And every fair from fair sometime declines,

By chance or nature's changing course untrimm'd;

But thy eternal summer shall not fade,

Nor lose possession of that fair thou ow'st;

Nor shall death brag thou wander'st in his shade,

When in eternal lines to time thou grow'st:

So long as men can breathe or eyes can see,

So long lives this, and this gives life to thee.

THEME

CREATING A LEGACY

William Shakespeare (1564–1616) wrote Sonnet 18 (of 154) as a love poem. But my focus in this legacy section is on what Shakespeare wrote in the last two lines:

So long as men can breathe or eyes can see,
So long lives this, and this gives life to thee.

Shakespeare makes the incredibly boastful claim that the loved one addressed in the poem will be immortal because of the words Shakespeare wrote. Since he is considered by many to be the greatest poet ever, Shakespeare's claim was really not far-fetched. We read his words today, 500 years later, and wonder who that mysterious person in the poem was.

How many of us will have something written about us that will be long remembered after death brags "we wander in his shade"? It's never too early to start thinking about how you will be remembered and for how long.

- Will you be remembered for your most glorious job title?
- Will you be remembered for all the material possessions you accumulated?
- Will you be remembered as a good person of character and honor, regardless of how much wealth or fame you gained?
- Will you be remembered for the positive accomplishments you achieved that made the world a little better place?

As my friend Jeff Powers once said,

You can leave a legacy, or you can leave a stain.

Too many of our leaders are leaving stains. Make sure what imperfections you have are small, that you seek forgiveness for your errors, and that your legacy is a positive inspiration to others. In so doing someone may write about you in words that echo over time as Shakespeare's Sonnet 18 does.

PRACTICAL APPLICATIONS

1. How will you be remembered?
2. Will you have made any lasting impact on some small piece of the world?
3. Reflect today on what you would like people to remember about you.
4. Then start working now to create that memorable legacy.

Leading a good life means creating a legacy people will long remember.

GREATER IN BATTLE

GAUTAMA BUDDHA

Greater in battle
than the man who would conquer
a thousand-thousand men,
is he who would conquer
just one-himself.
Better to conquer yourself
than others.
When you've trained yourself,
living in constant self-control,
neither a deva [deity] nor gandhabba [heavenly musician],
nor a Mara [demon] banded with Brahmas[gods],
could turn that triumph
back into defeat.

THEME

CONQUERING YOURSELF

Gautama Buddha was a sage in India who founded Buddhism. He lived between the sixth and fourth centuries BCE. Buddha means "awakened one" or "enlightened one."[34]

David Brooks, a *New York Times* journalist, writes persuasively in his 2015 book *The Road to Character* about two opposing sides of human nature, which he dubs Adam I and Adam II. Adam I symbolizes our "resume virtues": our career-oriented, ambitious side, that wants to build and create, seek status and victories. Adam II symbolizes our "eulogy virtues": our moral side, that seeks inner character with a solid sense of right and wrong, that wants to serve a higher purpose. Brooks posits that we live in the contradiction between Adam I and Adam II, vacillating between the two sides of ourselves. Brooks' "road to character" advocates more of an Adam II life.

Buddha understood this wisdom thousands of years before Brooks. The leader conquering a "thousand-thousand" is Brooks' Adam I. The leader who conquers himself is Adam II, and that "triumph" cannot be overturned by deities, heavenly bodies, or even good angels banded with bad angels. Brooks' Adam II is the ultimate quest.

I spent thirty years in the business world seeking a better way to lead. I was Adam I, driven and rightly proud of the accomplishments we made as colleagues. Slowly, I learned about better ways to lead, all of which involved invoking my Adam II. When I "retired" to the Rocky Mountains of Colorado, I wasn't satisfied filling all my days with golfing or skiing. I wanted to serve a higher purpose, so I began sharing what I had learned through teaching, writing, and speaking.

Then it dawned on me: all that came before in my business career was prelude and preparation for the work I do now, my true Adam II self, where I contribute to the intellectual capital on leadership, and, even more important, perhaps change a few hearts and minds about leadership. Adam II expressions of yourself are a much better legacy to leave.

PRACTICAL APPLICATIONS

1. Will your work primarily influence your resume virtues or your eulogy virtues?

2. Are you seeking status and victories or inner character, serving a noble purpose?

3. What might you do starting today to travel down the road to character?

Good leaders garner eulogies to their legacies that eclipse their resume accomplishments.

IN FLANDERS FIELDS

DR. JOHN MCCRAE

In Flanders fields the poppies blow
Between the crosses, row on row,
That mark our place; and in the sky
The larks, still bravely singing, fly
Scarce heard amid the guns below.
We are the Dead. Short days ago
We lived, felt dawn, saw sunset glow,
Loved and were loved, and now we lie
In Flanders fields.
Take up our quarrel with the foe:
To you from failing hands we throw
The torch; be yours to hold it high.
If ye break faith with us who die
We shall not sleep, though poppies grow.
In Flanders fields.

THEME

PASSING YOUR TORCH

Lieutenant Colonel John McCrae (1872–1918) was a Canadian poet, physician, and soldier who died during World War I. He wrote "In Flanders Fields" in 1915 about a region in Belgium on the Western Front, a beleaguered area that agonizingly suffered horrendous trench warfare over four torturous years. After a close friend was killed in battle, McCrae performed the burial service and noted how quickly poppies grew around the graves. He then wrote his famous poem while sitting in the back of an ambulance.[35]

The lesson I derive from this poem is that sometimes those who undertake great endeavors do not survive to see the fruits of their efforts. In building the great cathedrals over decades, or even centuries, the architects, stonemasons, and other artisans involved knew the work would not be completed in their lifetimes. Yet they threw themselves into their work wholeheartedly. Then it was up to those who followed those early pioneers to carry on the noble work.

Sometimes the work I undertook in my career was interrupted because forces moved me onto a different path. My work at Monarch Marking Systems in Dayton, Ohio, was the best job I ever had, but when my boss, Tom Loemker, asked me to help him at corporate HQ, our family had to move again and start anew.

Each of us can only advance the cause so far. Then, it's up to those who follow, those we've led, developed, inspired, and unleashed as leaders to carry on. They'll take the torch we throw to them and hold it high, so we may rest in peace in Flanders Fields.

PRACTICAL APPLICATIONS

1. Are you likely to achieve all those noble dreams you had in youth?
2. If not, then to whom will you throw your torches?
3. What are their names?
4. Have you fully prepared them to carry on, developing them as character-based leaders committed to the cause you have worked for?
5. If not, what more might you do starting today to ensure they carry on your work?

Leading well means unleashing others to carry high your torch.

MAY IT PLEASE YOUR HONOR

SUSAN B. ANTHONY

Judge:

"The sentence of the Court is that you pay a fine of one hundred dollars and the costs of the prosecution."

Miss Anthony:

"May it please your honor, I shall never pay a dollar of your unjust penalty. All the stock in trade I possess is a $10,000 debt, incurred by publishing my paper-The Revolution-four years ago, the sole object of which was to educate all women to do precisely as I have done, rebel against your man-made, unjust, unconstitutional forms of law, that tax, fine, imprison and hang women, while they deny them the right of representation in the government; and I shall work on with might and main to pay every dollar of that honest debt, but not a penny shall go to this unjust claim. And I shall earnestly and persistently continue to urge all women to the practical recognition of the old revolutionary maxim, that 'Resistance to tyranny is obedience to God.'"

THEME

RESISTING INJUSTICE

Susan B. Anthony (1820–1906) was an American social reformer. She was a major force in the women's suffrage movement in the United States during the late nineteenth and early twentieth centuries in order to gain the right to vote for women.

In 1873, after being found guilty of the "crime" of voting without that explicit right, Anthony stoically replied with the famous remarks above. (Since there is no transcript of the trial remarks, there are several different versions of her exact comments.[36]) In 1878 Anthony and her fellow suffragette, Elizabeth Cady Stanton, arranged for Congress to be presented with an amendment giving women the right to vote. But it was not until 1920 that it finally became the nineteenth Amendment to the U.S. Constitution.

Injustice must be challenged. Anthony and her colleagues spent decades bravely fighting for a right so fundamental that we now virtually take it for granted. They were lonely and ostracized. They endured hardships, ridicule, personal insults, family ostracism, and even jail. Yet they remained undaunted in their work.

Can you imagine the courage it took to do this work, for this woman to make this speech to a courtroom judge? Anthony's courage came from the core belief that a gross injustice needed to be corrected.

During my career, I often fought to instill ethical behavior in organizations. At times, I heard from naysayers that this fight was like Don Quixote "tilting at windmills." There will always be greedy or evil people imposing injustices on others. Indeed, we can't change human nature, but we can influence human behavior. That's what good leadership is all about, being exemplars for a better brand of leadership.

So, regardless of the odds against them, and the personal prices that must be paid, leaders fight to rectify injustices.

PRACTICAL APPLICATIONS

1. Do you see injustices around you?
2. Are you prepared to stand against them, regardless of the cost?
3. What might you do today to take a stand for what's right?

Good leaders resist injustices, fighting for what's right.

NEVER GIVE IN

WINSTON CHURCHILL

This is the lesson: never give in, never give in, never, never, never, never-in nothing, great or small, large or petty-never give in except to convictions of honor and good sense.

Never yield to force; never yield to the apparently overwhelming might of the enemy

...

Very different is the mood today. Britain, other nations thought, had drawn a sponge across her slate. But instead our country stood in the gap. There was no flinching and no thought of giving in; and by what seemed almost a miracle to those outside these Islands, though we ourselves never doubted it, we now find ourselves in a position where I say that we can be sure that we have only to persevere to conquer.

THEME

NEVER GIVING IN

Prime Minister of Great Britain, Sir Winston Churchill (1874–1965), was a British statesman widely regarded as one of the greatest wartime leaders of the twentieth century. He visited his alma mater, The Harrow School, on October 29, 1941. These excerpts from his remarks to the students show his unrelenting resolve to "never give in, never give in, never, never, never, never."

Churchill's stirring phrases echo what he had said a few months before to the British House of Commons in 1940:

We shall go on to the end. We shall fight in France, we shall fight on the seas and oceans, we shall fight with growing confidence and growing strength in the air, we shall defend our island, whatever the cost may be. We shall fight on the beaches; we shall fight on the landing grounds; we shall fight in the fields and in the streets; we shall fight in the hills; we shall never surrender.

Can you imagine being a Brit huddled around the radio some dark night, listening to Churchill's stirring words while the blitz bombs were falling all around London? Many experts and foreign government leaders thought that Britain's chance to survive the Nazi onslaught were nil: a sponge (eraser) had been wiped across her slate (blackboard).

But Churchill's unrelenting resolve almost singlehandedly held together the hopes of the British people in their darkest days fighting against Nazi Germany. The responsibility of leadership is never to give in to evil. "Never, never, never, never."

You may have to revise or abandon your career plans or business strategy if you see things are not working out. You may have to leave that job in an unethical organization that is entrenched in their immoral ways. But when you encounter evil in the world, you must take a stand, even if you must do it alone.

PRACTICAL APPLICATIONS

1. To what challenge in your life must you never give in?
2. What can you do starting today to strengthen your resolve to never give in on this challenge?

Leading well means never giving in to evil. Never.

THIS IS THE TRUE JOY IN LIFE

GEORGE BERNARD SHAW

This is the true joy in life,

The being used for a purpose recognized by yourself as a mighty one;

The being thoroughly worn out before you are thrown on the scrap heap;

The being a force of nature instead of a feverish, selfish little clod of ailments and grievances,

Complaining that the world will not devote itself to making you happy.

I am of the opinion that my life belongs to the whole community,

And as long as I live, it is my privilege to do for it whatever I can.

I want to be thoroughly used up when I die,

For the harder I work, the more I live.

I rejoice in life for its own sake.

Life is no brief candle to me.

It is sort of a splendid torch, which I've got a hold of for the moment,

And I want to make it burn as brightly as possible

Before handing it on to future generations.

THEME

BURNING YOUR TORCH BRIGHTLY

Nobel Laureate George Bernard Shaw (1856–1950) was an Irish playwright and co-founder of the London School of Economics. He wrote "This Is the True Joy in Life" in a dedication to his play *Man and Superman* in 1903. In it, Shaw addresses the theme of how we find true joy in our lives.

Each of us is entitled to find some joy in life. Yes, life also involves suffering. But joy can make the suffering more bearable, so we must understand where joy comes from.

Shaw writes that true joy in life is found by throwing oneself thoroughly into a mighty purpose, even to the extent that you'll be thoroughly worn out at life's end. Shaw directly contradicts Shakespeare's lament in *Macbeth* that says:

> *Out, out, brief candle!*
> *Life's but a walking shadow, a poor player,*
> *That struts and frets his hour upon the stage,*
> *And then is heard no more. It is a tale*
> *Told by an idiot, full of sound and fury,*
> *Signifying nothing.*

Our lives should not be brief candles, unremembered after we pass, except as "little clods of ailments and grievances." We should contribute to the "whole community" through our families, friends, neighborhoods, social causes, and our work, whatever it may be, to make a difference with our lives.

Our legacies should be to burn the splendid torches of our lives as brightly as possible before we pass our contributions on to future generations.

PRACTICAL APPLICATIONS

1. Regardless of your circumstances, will your life be a brief candle of ailments and grievances, or a splendid torch?
2. How might you make your torch burn more brightly today by throwing yourself into a mighty purpose?

Finding true joy in life means burning your torch brightly for a mighty purpose.

THE HARDER THE CONFLICT

THOMAS PAINE

The harder the conflict, the more glorious the triumph. What we obtain too cheap, we esteem too lightly; it is dearness only that gives everything its value. I love the man that can smile in trouble, that can gather strength from distress and grow brave by reflection. 'Tis the business of little minds to shrink; but he whose heart is firm, and whose conscience approves his conduct, will pursue his principles unto death.

THEME

STRIVING VALIANTLY

Thomas Paine (1737–1809) was an English-American political activist and one of the Founding Fathers of the United States. He authored two influential pamphlets in 1776, inspiring the patriot rebels to declare America's independence from Britain.

Paine's message is that leaders are willing to undertake noble, difficult, even impossible-seeming challenges. Not all leadership involves those challenging conflicts. Many people lead in less than death-defying circumstances:

- The single mom who works two jobs to pay the bills and always shows up every day to help her child with homework.

- The teacher who buys school supplies, food, and a warm jacket out of her own pocket for needy kids and drives into the "hood" to get their parents and grand-parents involved.

- The tech analyst who expresses his concern about how a downsizing is being handled, prompting senior leaders to reassess their approach.

All these are leadership in action. Great work.

But sometimes, wanted or not, a clarion call sounds for someone who may choose to rise to the occasion, someone with a firm heart and a principled conscience. That person may someday be you. How can you be prepared to step up? How can you decide whether to undertake this challenging conflict?

If you reflect on what leadership involves, if you understand that you are a latent leader, even without position or title, then you can assess the potentially glorious triumph. If the cause is worth the effort, if the cause is noble and right, if the other options have been exhausted, then it may be time for you to step up, answer the call, and lead. Win or lose, you'll leave a legacy you can be proud of.

PRACTICAL APPLICATIONS

1. Is there a noble cause that needs to be undertaken in your organization?

2. Is it time for you to step up and be a leader?

Good leaders strive valiantly for worthy causes.

FOUNDERS' WISDOM

AUTHORS: VARIOUS

From the Declaration of Independence:

We hold these truths to be self-evident, that all men are created equal, that they are endowed by their Creator with certain unalienable Rights, that among these are Life, Liberty and the pursuit of Happiness.-That to secure these rights, Governments are instituted among Men, deriving their just powers from the consent of the governed

...

And for the support of this Declaration, with a firm reliance on the protection of Divine Providence, we mutually pledge to each other our Lives, our Fortunes, and our sacred Honor.

Preamble to the Constitution:

We the People of the United States, in Order to form a more perfect Union, establish Justice, insure domestic Tranquility, provide for the common defence, promote the general Welfare, and secure the Blessings of Liberty to ourselves and our Posterity, do ordain and establish this Constitution for the United States of America.

From the Bill of Rights:

First Amendment

Congress shall make no law respecting an establishment of religion, or prohibiting the free exercise thereof; or abridging the freedom of speech, or of the press; or the right of the people peaceably to assemble, and to petition the government for a redress of grievances.

Tenth Amendment

The powers not delegated to the United States by the Constitution, nor prohibited by it to the states, are reserved to the states respectively, or to the people.

THEME

CREATING A NEW COUNTRY

The Founding Fathers of the United States were learned gentlemen who met over a series of years to draft defining documents for governing a new country. Many of these documents became examples for other nascent nations as they developed their own sets of governing documents. The Declaration of Independence (1776) was drafted primarily by Thomas Jefferson and then edited by the Continental Congress. The Constitution (1789) and Bill of Rights (1791), which comprises the first ten amendments to the Constitution, were drafted primarily by James Madison with vigorous debate and input from various committees of the assembled delegates.

Currently, it is in vogue to cite the many failures and deficiencies of the United States. And certainly, America has much to be ashamed of: Founders who were slave-owning, property owners; basic civil rights denied far too long to minorities and women; atrocities committed against Native Americans; greedy capitalists and robber barons who exploited people and natural resources; cartels and monopolies that extracted egregious profits; resistance to many essential social reforms; CIA over-reach in foreign countries; environmental degradation; government and corporate scandals; and even wars fought for what seem like questionable purposes in hindsight. The United States is certainly far from a perfect country.

But I challenge anyone to give me one persuasive example of another major country that has done more good for the world. We have sacrificed our sons and daughters in wars against evil oppressors, helped foreign adversaries to rebuild, given great time and financial assistance to help those in need, and taken in countless immigrants fleeing oppression or seeking a better life. We have raised millions of people from poverty in our own country with an admittedly imperfect, regulated, and market-based economic system (versus a government-planned economy) that fuels the social safety nets to provide for those in need.

I consider our Founders, with all their flaws, to be people of honor who deserve respect. How many of us today would pledge "our lives, our fortunes, and our sacred honor" for our country? Too few, I fear. These excerpts from our most important documents give testimony to the noble ideas and dreams of America's Founding Fathers.

John Adams, who was one of the Founders, once said,

> *Posterity, you will never know how much it cost the present generation*
> *to preserve your freedom! I hope you will make a good use of it.*

PRACTICAL APPLICATIONS

1. Take a moment today to honor the legacy the Founding Fathers of the United States left in establishing America.
2. Consider what you might do today to further their legacy.

Good leaders, like America's Founders, leave an impressive and lasting legacy.

THE FINAL INSPECTION

JOSHUA HELTERBRAN

The soldier stood and faced God
Which must always come to pass,
He hoped his shoes were shining,
Just as brightly as his brass.

"Step forward now, you soldier,
How shall I deal with you?
Have you always turned the other cheek?
To My Church have you been true?"

The soldier squared his shoulders and
said, "No, Lord, I guess I ain't,
Because those of us who carry guns,
Can't always be a saint.

I've had to work most Sundays,
And at times my talk was tough,
And sometimes I've been violent,
Because the world is awfully rough.

But, I never took a penny
That wasn't mine to keep...
Though I worked a lot of overtime
When the bills got just too steep.

And I never passed a cry for help,
Though at times I shook with fear,
And sometimes, God forgive me,
I've wept unmanly tears.

I know I don't deserve a place
Among the people here,
They never wanted me around,
Except to calm their fears.

If you've a place for me here, Lord,
It needn't be so grand,
I never expected or had too much,
But if you don't, I'll understand."

There was silence all around the throne,
Where the saints had often trod,
As the soldier waited quietly,
For the judgment of his God.

"Step forward now, you soldier,
You've borne your burdens well,
Walk peacefully on Heaven's streets,
You've done your time in Hell."
...

THEME

REWARDING GOOD LEADERS

U. S. Army Sergeant Joshua Helterbran (1978–) served his country as a Ranger in Panama, Kosovo, Bosnia, and in Iraq where he was wounded. He has since recovered and is currently serving in the Iowa National Guard. "The Final Inspection" resonates with me because we often, hypocritically, expect our leaders to be perfect. But we also know that leadership is just plain hard. Leaders make mistakes because they are human.

Like Helterbran's soldier facing God, there are times when each of us can look down at our shoes and soulfully confess our mistakes. Sometimes, though, we can let that guilt pervade our lives, dragging us down in shame and sorrow, surrounding us with a negative aura that discourages others.

I can certainly recall many mistakes I made during my career. I don't regret too much the strategic or tactical mistakes. Those mistakes were ones that we could normally recover from with rapid mid-course corrections.

The ones I do regret were the people mistakes I made: how I treated others, how I let my own insecurities and impatience lead me to be less than the person I should have been. Hopefully, those whom I offended or hurt will look at my total life in context and forgive me for mistakes and focus instead on the good that I did and the intentions I had in my work.

And I trust that a loving God, whatever that higher power might be in all its mystery, will look at the total context of our lives, including mine, and let those who have led and served well find comfort and peace in a better place.

PRACTICAL APPLICATIONS

1. In total context, even though you've not been perfect, have you served and led well?

2. Can you let go of the guilt and shame you may feel for the mistakes you've made, learning from them to be a better person?

3. What can you begin doing today to ensure you "walk peacefully on Heaven's streets"?

Good leaders aren't perfect, but they serve with honor.

LONG WALK TO FREEDOM

NELSON MANDELA

A garden was one of the few things in prison that one could control. To plant a seed, watch it grow, to tend it and then harvest it, offered a simple but enduring satisfaction. The sense of being the custodian of this small patch of earth offered a taste of freedom.

In some ways, I saw the garden as a metaphor for certain aspects of my life. A leader must also tend his garden; he, too, plants seeds, and then watches, cultivates, and harvests the results. Like the gardener, a leader must take responsibility for what he cultivates; he must mind his work, try to repel enemies, preserve what can be preserved, and eliminate what cannot succeed.

THEME

CULTIVATING A GARDEN

Nelson Mandela (1918–2013) was president of South Africa from 1994 to 1999. He was the first president of that country to be selected by a fully representative election. He came to prominence through his anti-apartheid positions. He served 27 years in prison for his revolutionary work, most of that time on Robben Island. Mandela wrote about leadership and gardens in his autobiography *Long Walk to Freedom*.

Like a gardener, a leader diligently plants seeds, nurtures them, weeds out harmful intruders, preserves the nurturing soil, and takes responsibility for the results. I have learned that leadership takes patience, not my strong suit early in life.

Some people believe organizational leaders can do whatever they wish and easily implement their desires. But organizations don't bend that way. Former U. S. President Richard Nixon (disgraced as he was for the Watergate cover-up) insightfully observed, referring to the bureaucracy of big organizations,

It is very interesting when I give an order and nothing happens.

Edicts from leaders will often be resisted, so seeds must be planted and carefully cultivated. Those who seek to undermine what the gardener wishes to grow must be persuaded, or compromised with, or helped to conform, or taken out of the garden.

Leadership is all about trusteeship, being a custodian, or steward for an organization, its tangible assets, and most of all its people. Control is an illusion when dealing with people. We have enough trouble controlling ourselves, let alone others.

The gardening metaphor is much more apt, especially if we view leadership as the act of many gardeners, not just one, in large and small greenhouses full of flowers, plants, bushes, and trees scattered around the world. In that sense leadership is a group performance in the greenhouses, ebbing and flowing amongst the many gardeners.

PRACTICAL APPLICATIONS

1. Are you cultivating a garden with your colleagues where their ideas, as well as yours, can grow and blossom?
2. What might you do today to plant some seeds to help your colleagues grow?

Good leaders cultivate people into blossoming gardens.

LIFE

CHARLOTTE BRONTE

Life, believe, is not a dream
So dark as sages say;

Oft a little morning rain
Foretells a pleasant day.

Sometimes there are clouds of gloom,
But these are transient all;

If the shower will make the roses bloom,
O why lament its fall?

Rapidly, merrily,
Life's sunny hours flit by,

Gratefully, cheerily
Enjoy them as they fly!

What though Death at times steps in,
And calls our Best away?

What though sorrow seems to win,
O'er hope, a heavy sway?

Yet Hope again elastic springs,
Unconquered, though she fell;

Still buoyant are her golden wings,
Still strong to bear us well.
Manfully, fearlessly,
The day of trial bear,

For gloriously, victoriously,
Can courage quell despair!

THEME

HAVING COURAGE

Charlotte Bronte (1816–1855), the eldest of the three Bronte sisters, was an English novelist and poet. She published "Life" in 1846, and then published *Jane Eyre*, her best known novel, in 1848 under the nom de plume "Currer Bell." In those days, female writers often kept their gender secret in order to get published.

In "Life," Bronte acknowledges all the woes of the human experience: gloomy clouds, rain, tribulations of all sorts, sorrow, and even death calling our best away. But she recognizes that it's the showers that make the roses bloom. How could we appreciate life's beauties if all were sublime? There must be storms for us to enjoy the sunshine. So, Bronte celebrates hope and courage: "Yet hope again elastic springs."

I share Bronte's celebration of life. With all the negative news of our 24/7 world, it's easy to get discouraged and slip into despair. But I'm an "optimistic-realist," as leaders must be. Leaders can't live in a world seen through rose-colored glasses. They must acknowledge reality. At the same time, though, leaders must offer hope to people for the future. Few will follow a negative or cynical mindset. I believe that we human beings create most of our own challenges. Therefore, I believe that we can solve them too-by working well together and leading better than we have. It just takes patience and courage to soldier on. As my friend Bob Whipple writes,

The absence of fear is the incubator of trust.

Courage is not the absence of fear. That's reckless foolhardiness. Courage is the will to proceed in spite of the fear with the hope and belief that the future we can create together can be brighter.

PRACTICAL APPLICATIONS

1. Is your focus primarily on the rainy days, or the sunny ones?
2. Do you have hope for the future, or are you a pessimist?
3. Can you think of at least three things today that will make your future brighter?
4. Then can you initiate some action today to make each of those three things more likely to happen, even if it takes some courage to begin?

Leading well means marshaling the courage to make the future brighter.

FINAL REFLECTIONS

Our journey through these poems, prose passages, speeches, and curious verses has drawn from authors and leaders around the globe, covering thousands of years, and has plumbed great wisdom. Yet, we have only scratched the surface of leadership. It's a subject much discussed and pursued but never completely mastered.

In Part I we explored themes on leading ourselves first:

- From Rudyard Kipling we learned that if others view you as a leader with character, you'll have willing and committed followers.

- Teddy Roosevelt inspired us to leap into the arena to fight for worthy causes instead of sniping from the grandstands.

- Paulo Coelho advised us to pursue our dreams and follow our hearts.

- Robert Frost counseled us to choose our roads wisely and to pause once in a while to admire our own snowy woods before moving forward to act.

- Wilferd Peterson encouraged us to slow down life's hectic pace.

- Don Schlitz wrote lyrics about wisely playing the hands we're dealt since every hand's a potential winner and a potential loser.

- Max Ehrmann told us that good leaders have an inner peace and presence that radiates from and resonates with people, drawing them closer.

- Carl Sandburg spoke of flexing between steel and velvet, the hard and soft edges of leadership, a leadership style exemplified by Abraham Lincoln.

- The Cherokee grandfather warned of the two wolves inside each of us and to be careful which one we feed.

- Shakespeare's *Hamlet* showed us the need to be decisive without vacillating.

- William Murray addressed the necessity of bold commitments.

- Edward Everett Hale encouraged us to do something, even if we have to act alone.

- Emily Dickinson echoed that same theme by showing all we need to do is help one other person.

- An unknown author reminded us that learning, feeling, changing, growing, and loving all involve risks. So does leadership.

- Edgar Guest encouraged us to persevere, even just one more day at a time, to capture the victor's cup.

- Psalm 23 helps us place our trust in a higher power, even in the "valley of the shadow of death."

- John Masefield showed us the need to find our own places of refuge to refresh the body, mind, and soul.

- Annie Dillard encouraged us to go deeper into the unknown where we are connected to the universe.
- David Whyte implored us to bring our souls to work where they can contribute to the collective soul of the organization.

In Part II we explored themes on leading others:

- Parker Palmer taught us about head and heart.
- Robert Greenleaf revealed that followers bestow leadership on those who serve them.
- Martin Luther King, Jr. used Jesus' Biblical words to reiterate that everybody can be great because everybody can serve.
- An unknown author showed us leaders are more effective when they learn to speak gently.
- C.J. Dennis helped us understand good leaders must make judgments without being superficially judgmental.
- J.K. Rowling, through the voice of Albus Dumbledore in *Harry Potter,* encouraged us to see beyond differences in people to achieve noble deeds together.
- Yehuda Amichai wrote that leaders aren't self-righteous. They are open-minded, willing, even anxious, to listen to and learn from others.
- Sydney Harris quoted St. Thomas Aquinas, who wisely said that to get others to follow, you need to start where they are.
- Shakespeare wrote about "trusting few," but I personally discovered that it isn't a good way to lead. Good leaders extend trust first.
- Gan Chennai compared trust with beliefs, showing that leaders build trust with people.
- Robert Service told us about keeping promises, even though sometimes doing so is difficult as in the cremation of Sam McGee.
- Lao-Tzu in the Tao taught that leading isn't about elevating oneself at other's expense. It's about elevating and honoring others so they feel "we did this ourselves."
- Victor Frankl showed that we can choose our attitude, regardless of the circumstances.
- Machiavelli counseled that, although it is difficult to do so, good leaders must challenge the status quo.
- Franklin Roosevelt spoke to us in his first inaugural address about the paralyzing effects of fear.

- John F. Kennedy spoke to us in his first inaugural address about rising to the higher standard of what we can do for our country.

- Christopher Logue revealed that leading effectively sometimes means giving people a push so they discover their true potential.

- Robert McNeish shared lessons from the geese showing that leading well means working together with your colleagues, even rotating the leadership.

- 1 Corinthians encouraged us to anchor our behavior in love.

- The 14th Dalai Lama showed us that good leaders connect with the souls of others through love and compassion.

- Demas Jasper illustrated through haiku that "leading true" means being an authentic leader with a moral compass.

- Shakespeare inspired us to share leadership by creating "bands of brothers" among colleagues.

- Richard Barrett encouraged us to let go of the ego and get into the flow of souls with others.

- J.R.R. Tolkien, through the voice of Eowyn in *The Return of the King,* showed us that, if we remove stereotypes, good leadership can emerge from anyone in the fellowship.

- Rumi encouraged us to take chances by weaning ourselves out of our comfort zones.

- Alfred Lord Tennyson taught us that leading well means caring for the well-being of those you lead.

- Jon Krakauer spoke to us of the tests to our moral principles under extreme duress.

- Marianne Williamson shared that living and leading well mean letting your own inner light shine through.

- An unknown author illustrated humorously that good leaders don't beat dead horses.

- David Halberstam wrote how leaders empower people to sometimes achieve an incredible state of flow.

- And Walt Whitman poignantly told the importance of honoring the influencers that have guided you.

In Part III we explored themes about leaving a leadership legacy:
- Lewis Carroll revealed that, while there may always be more Jabberwocks to slay, your leadership calling is to take up your quests.

- Bessie Stanley advised that leading and living a good life mean being wise in how you define success.

- Percy Bysshe Shelley showed us our acquired trappings and monuments don't measure the quality of our lives. Humility, not hubris, is essential in leadership.

- Robert Kennedy counseled us that leading well means making ripples.

- Edgar Guest reminded us that leading well means being an exemplary role model, especially for children whose eyes are always on us.

- Kent Keith wrote that leading well means listening to your conscience, regardless of how others react, and just doing good anyway.

- Abraham Lincoln reminded us that good leaders acknowledge and carry on the best of their predecessors.

- William Shakespeare in his Sonnet 18 showed us that leading a good life means creating a legacy people will long remember.

- John McCrae, a soldier/doctor, wrote about ensuring that there are others to carry forth your torch.

- Susan B. Anthony inspired us to resist injustice and fight for what's right.

- Winston Churchill insisted that leading well means never giving in to evil. Never.

- George Bernard Shaw said that finding true joy in life means burning your torch brightly for a mighty purpose.

- The Founding Fathers of America designed a country that, even with all its faults, is still a beacon of hope and freedom in our troubled world.

- Joshua Helterbran, a soldier, showed us that good leaders, while not perfect, serve with honor.

- Nelson Mandela wrote that good leaders cultivate people into blossoming gardens.

- And Charlotte Bronte wrote that leading well means marshaling the courage to make the future brighter together.

I encourage each of you to find your own poems, short stories, speech or prose excerpts, or even song lyrics that resonate with your leadership style. Read them, and memorize those you really like. Discuss them with your family and colleagues occasionally to tease out the practical applications you can use, just as we have done throughout this book. Then those inspiring insights will be yours, not mine, and that will "make all the difference."

Leadership is complicated. It has been observed and studied throughout history, yet it is still misunderstood. It certainly was a mystery to me over many decades. So, perhaps we need to make it simpler, to return to the basics that the poets have shared with us?

Good leadership is not about fear, control, power, ego, manipulation, selfishness, or material success. Good leadership is harmonious with leading a good life. For our last quote, author and Pulitzer Prize winner Anna Quindlen (1953–) says in her 2000 commencement address at Villanoa University,

> So here is what I want to tell you today: Get a life.
>
> A real life, not a manic pursuit of the next promotion,
>
> the bigger paycheck, the larger house
>
> ...
>
> Get a life in which you are not alone.
>
> Find people you love, and who love you.

In the spirit of this book, even though I'm certainly not qualified as a poet, I'll take a risk and close with my own poem, briefly summarizing our journey with the sages:

Good luck and Godspeed on your leadership quest.

TO LEAD WELL

BOB VANOUREK

I'll start within,
Cultivating quality character,
Acting with integrity,
Listening with my heart,
Composed amid chaos,
A soul flooding forth with love.

I'll reach out,
Caring and connecting,
Serving,
Engendering trust,
Building relationships,
Unleashing others who soar.

I'll step up,
Saying "Yes,"
Choosing wisely,
Embracing change,
Striving for what's right,
Pursuing our dreams.

I'll leave a legacy,
A team of partners,
Companions with courage and character,
Leading and following,
Creators of worthy deeds,
Together undaunted.

APPENDIX 1

CLOSING LINES FROM EACH SECTION

This Appendix was inspired by my friend John Balkcom, who gathered the closing lines of each section to recapture the leadership messages we have read.

Leading Yourself

- If strong character forms the basis of your leadership, you will have willing and committed followers.
- Leading well means having the courage to fight for worthy causes.
- Leading yourself well means pursuing the dream your heart whispers.
- Leading your life well means being thoughtful about the roads you choose.
- When under extreme stress, good leaders pause to renew themselves, and then they act.
- Good leaders know they need to slow their pace at times.
- Leading well means making winners from whatever hands you're dealt.
- Good leaders conquer their egos.
- Good leaders learn to balance between their emotional and logical minds.
- Good leaders have an inner peace and presence that radiates out, resonating with people and drawing them close.
- Leading well means flexing between the hard and soft edges of leadership.
- Good leadership begins with the thoughts you choose to feed.
- When the pressure is on, good leaders are decisive.
- Leading well requires making bold commitments.
- Good leadership involves captaining your own ship to master your fate.
- Leading well means doing whatever you can do, even if the cause seems daunting.
- Helping even just one other person is good leadership.
- Good leadership involves overcoming our natural fears and taking risks.
- Good leaders persevere.
- Leading well often involves trusting a higher power.
- Leading well means refreshing in places of sanctuary.
- Good leaders connect with others.
- Good leaders bring their souls into their work, contributing to the collective soul of their organizations.

Leading Others

- Leading well means hiring and promoting for head and heart.
- Followers bestow leadership on those who serve them.
- Leading well means understanding your role is to serve others.
- Good leaders have learned to speak more gently.
- Good leaders make judgments without being superficially judgmental.
- Good leaders bridge factions.
- Good leaders aren't self-righteous. They are open-minded, willing, even anxious, to listen and learn from the views of others.
- To get people to follow you, you need to start where they are.
- Good leaders overcome their fear to trust.
- Good leaders go first in building smart trust with people.
- Good leaders keep their explicit and implicit promises.
- Leading people well is about elevating and honoring others so they can feel "we did this ourselves."
- Leading well means choosing an optimistic, loving attitude regardless of the circumstances.
- Good leaders challenge the status quo.
- Good leaders take vigorous action in adversity.
- Good leaders challenge others to higher standards.
- Leading well sometimes means calling people to the edge and giving them a push to discover they can fly.
- Leading well means working together, sharing leadership, and encouraging each other.
- Leading well means anchoring your behavior in love.
- Good leaders are compassionate.
- Leading well means being an authentic leader with a "true north" moral compass.
- Inspiring leadership creates "bands of brothers" among colleagues.
- Good leaders connect at a deep level with the souls of others.
- Good leaders will emerge from many places in your fellowship.
- Leading well and living well mean taking chances to venture forth.
- Leading well means caring for the well-being of those you lead.
- Good leaders have an intense desire to succeed but not at the expense of their ethical values.
- Living and leading well mean letting your own inner light shine through.

- Good leaders acknowledge reality, dismount dead horses, and ride mounts that will get them where they want to go.
- Good leaders radically empower people to achieve an incredible state of flow.
- Leading well involves honoring the influencers who have guided you.

Leaving a Leadership Legacy

- Good leaders pursue noble quests.
- Leading well and living a good life mean being wise in how you define success.
- Humility, not hubris, is essential in good leadership.
- Leading well means making ripples.
- Leading well means being an exemplary role model.
- Leading well means listening to your conscience and just doing good anyway.
- Good leaders acknowledge and carry on the best of their predecessors.
- Leading a good life means creating a legacy people will long remember.
- Good leaders garner eulogies to their legacies that eclipse their resume accomplishments.
- Leading well means unleashing others to carry high your torch.
- Good leaders resist injustices, fighting for what's right.
- Leading well means never giving in to evil. Never.
- Finding true joy in life means burning your torch brightly for a mighty purpose.
- Good leaders strive valiantly for worthy causes.
- Good leaders, like America's Founders, leave an impressive and lasting legacy.
- Good leaders aren't perfect, but they serve with honor.
- Good leaders cultivate people into blossoming gardens.
- Leading well means marshaling the courage to make the future brighter.

APPENDIX 2

OTHER GREAT WORKS

Literature is rich with many poems and prose passages that touch on leadership. But due to copyright restrictions, or the excessive costs of obtaining certain copyright permissions, I was unable to include some insightful verses in this book. I mention them here in brief passing to ignite your curiosity.

Fulghum Robert Lee Fulghum (1937–) is an American author and a Unitarian minister. His 1988 book of essays, *All I Really Need to Know I Learned in Kindergarten,* was a *New York Times* best seller for over two years. Often the heart of wisdom can be found in rediscovering the magic of the simple precepts we learned as children.

King Dr. Martin Luther King, Jr. (1929–1968) wrote his "Letter from Birmingham Jail" in 1963, defending the strategy of nonviolent resistance to racism. Like Susan B. Anthony's response to the judge in her trial for voting without that explicit right, King argued in his Birmingham Jail letter that nonviolent, civil disobedience is justified in the face of unjust laws.

King spoke his "I have a dream speech" in 1963 to a crowd of 250,000 people on the steps of the Lincoln Memorial in Washington DC. That speech was a defining moment in the American Civil Rights movement and is a wonderful example of a vision statement that a leader should frame. In his "Dream" speech, King elicited visions, sounds, and feelings, tapping into the senses of his audience. His stirring call for equal rights and freedom for African Americans resonated across the land and was a driving force in the Civil Rights Act of 1965. If you want to write a vision statement that galvanizes your colleagues, you have no better place to look for your inspiration than MLK's "I have a dream" speech.

Oliver Mary Oliver (1935–) is an American poet who has won the National Book Award and the Pulitzer Prize for poetry. Her wonderful poem "When Death Comes" echoes George Bernard Shaw's poem on living your life fully. She closes her poem with the line, "I don't want to end up simply having visited this world." It's worth reading her entire poem.

Seuss Theodor Seuss Geisel (1904–1991) was an American writer and illustrator best known for authoring children's books under the pen name Dr. Seuss. *Oh, The Places You'll Go* was published in 1990. His message in these whimsical rhymes comes down to believing in yourself and the future you can create. It's the opposite of being a victim, feeling the deck is stacked against you, whining and moaning about how unfair life may be. Leading well and living a joyful life means believing in yourself.

Unknown The author of a moving poem called "Scared to Trust" can't be determined with certainty. She may be writing under a pseudonym, and I don't wish to identify her and cause further pain. This author suffered through repeated sexual abuse as a youth and writes poignantly about her anguished suffering, the lack of justice, suicide, cutting herself, and more. One's heart breaks for the pain she has endured. Her closing line reprises the title: "I'm too scared to trust."

When I was hurt in life, I learned that to live a quality life and to lead others effectively I had to overcome my fear to trust and begin extending some "smart trust." I fervently hope the author of "Scared to Trust" finds some people she can trust in her life.

Gibran Kahlil Gibran (1883–1931) was a Lebanese-American artist, poet, and writer, who wrote in both Arabic and English. He is chiefly known for his 1923 best-selling book *The Prophet*. He was raised as a Christian, but was greatly influenced by Islam, especially Sufi mysticism.[37]

This passage is a verse from *The Prophet*:

> *... the erect and the fallen are but one man standing in twilight*
> *between the night of his pigmy-self and the day of his god-self ...*

The message to me is that each of us, as in the Cherokee's "Two Wolves" story, has the potential for both good and evil within. We love to deny this reality, thinking the bad guys have some deficiency that leads to their crimes, while we are all fine and upstanding (except for a few minor faults of course). But that thought process is a delusion.

Philip Zimbardo in his chilling and groundbreaking book, *The Lucifer Effect*, shows that all of us have the potential, in certain circumstances, under certain pressures, to do bad deeds. In *The Lucifer Effect* he recounts (among many other fascinating studies) the 1971 Stanford University prison experiment on graduate students, randomly cast as either prisoners or prison guards. The students designated as guards soon "enforced authoritarian measures and ultimately subjected some of the prisoners to psychological torture ... and the entire experiment was abruptly stopped..."[38]

So, regardless of your genes and parenting, or lack of parenting, believe that within you lie both great gifts to share as well as loathsome lies. We need to choose wisely.

Leading from Within: Poetry That Sustains the Courage to Lead Not many books have been written about poetry, great literature, and leadership. One notable exception which I wish to acknowledge as an inspiration is *Leading from Within: Poetry That Sustains the Courage to Lead*. This wonderful 2007 compendium, edited by Sam M. Intrator and Megan Scribner, is a collection of the favorite poems and commentaries from luminaries such as Madeline Albright, Parker Palmer, Robert F. Kennedy, Peter Senge, Bill White, James Autry, L. J. Rittenhouse, Billy Shore, John Bogle, and many more. If you have enjoyed *Leadership Wisdom*, I recommend this repository of wisdom as well.

Perhaps you have some other favorite poems or prose passages that touch on leadership and would like to recommend them? If so, please email me at bobvanourek@comcast.net. Maybe we'll create a sequel?

ENDNOTES

1. Anderson, Hitlin, and Atkinson, "Wikipedia at 15: Millions of readers in scores of languages," Pew Research Center, January 14, 2016, last accessed January 19, 2016, http://www.pewresearch.org/fact–tank/2016/01/14/wikipedia–at–15/?utm_source=Pew+Research+Center&utm_campaign=5e59eb8ed6–Weekly_Jan_14_20161_13_2016&utm_medium=email&utm_term=0_3e953b9b70–5e59eb8ed6–399832305.

2. Mihai Andrei, "Study shows Wikipedia Accuracy is 99.5%, ZME Science, September 25, 2014, last accessed January 19, 2016, http://www.zmescience.com/science/study–wikipedia–25092014/

3. "The Road Not Taken," Wikipedia contributors, *Wikipedia, The Free Encyclopedia,* date of last revision December 17, 2015. Last accessed January 19, 2016. https://en.wikipedia.org/w/index.php?title=The_Road_Not_Taken&oldid=695580107. Primary contributors: Revision history statistics. Page version ID: 695580107.

4. "Stopping by Wood on a Snowy Evening," Wikipedia contributors, *Wikipedia, The Free Encyclopedia,* date of last revision December 29, 2015. Last accessed January 19, 2016. https://en.wikipedia.org/w/index.php?title=Stopping_by_Woods_on_a_Snowy_Evening&oldid=697250607. Primary contributors: Revision history statistics. Page version ID: 697250607.

5. "Wilferd Arlan Peterson," Wikipedia contributors, *Wikipedia, The Free Encyclopedia,* date of last revision October 24, 2015. Last accessed January 19, 2016. https://en.wikipedia.org/w/index.php?title=Wilferd_Arlan_Peterson&oldid=687215488. Primary contributors: Revision history statistics. Page version ID: 687215488.

6. "Slow Me Down Lord," A–Spiritual–Journey–of–healing, http://www.a–spiritual–journey–of–healing.com/slow–me–down–lord.html. Last accessed January 19, 2016.

7. "Casey at the Bat," Wikipedia contributors, *Wikipedia, The Free Encyclopedia,* date of last revision January 18, 2016. Last accessed January 19, 2016. https://en.wikipedia.org/w/index.php?title=Casey_at_the_Bat&oldid=700515857. Primary contributors: Revision history statistics. Page version ID: 700515857.

8. "Ernest Thayer," Wikipedia contributors, *Wikipedia, The Free Encyclopedia,* date of last revision January 19, 2016. Last accessed January 19, 2016. https://en.wikipedia.org/w/index.php?title=Ernest_Thayer&oldid=700565356. Primary contributors: Revision history statistics. Page version ID: 700565356.

9. "Carl Sandberg," Wikipedia contributors, *Wikipedia, The Free Encyclopedia,* date of last revision January 17, 2016. Last accessed January 19, 2016. https://en.wikipedia.org/w/index.php?title=Carl_Sandburg&oldid=700241092. Primary contributors: Revision history statistics. Page version ID: 700241092.

10. Bob and Gregg Vanourek, *Triple Crown Leadership: Building Excellent, Ethical, and Enduring Organizations,* McGraw–Hill, 2012. See pages 83–103 for a fuller discussion of steel and velvet.

11. "William Shakespeare," Wikipedia contributors, *Wikipedia, The Free Encyclopedia,* date of last revision January 16, 2016. Last accessed January 19, 2016. https://en.wikipedia.org/w/index.php?title=William_Shakespeare&oldid=700142540. Primary contributors: Revision history statistics. Page version ID: 700142540.

12. "Emily Dickinson," Wikipedia contributors, *Wikipedia, The Free Encyclopedia,* date of last revision January 19, 2016. Last accessed January 19, 2016. https://en.wikipedia.org/w/index.php?title=Emily_Dickinson&oldid=700631527. Primary contributors: Revision history statistics. Page version ID: 700631527.

13. "William Arthur Ward," Wikipedia contributors, *Wikipedia, The Free Encyclopedia,* date of last revision August 14, 2015. Last accessed January 19, 2016. https://en.wikipedia.org/w/index.php?title=William_Arthur_Ward&oldid=676008335. Primary contributors: Revision history statistics. Page version ID: 676008335.

14. "Edgar Guest," Wikipedia contributors, *Wikipedia, The Free Encyclopedia,* date of last revision January 18, 2016. Last accessed January 19, 2016. https://en.wikipedia.org/w/index.php?title=Edgar_Guest&oldid=700387478. Primary contributors: Revision history statistics. Page version ID: 700387478.

15. "Psalm 23," Wikipedia contributors, *Wikipedia, The Free Encyclopedia,* date of last revision December 29, 2015. Last accessed January 19, 2016. https://en.wikipedia.org/w/index.php?title=Psalm_23&oldid=697352315. Primary contributors: Revision history statistics. Page version ID: 697352315.

16. L.J. Rittenhouse, "Interview with Parker Palmer" in *Executive Talent,* Spring 2001, last accessed January 19, 2016, http://www.couragerenewal.org/PDFs/rittenhouse-leading_from_the_heart.pdf

17. Amy Adkins, "Majority of U.S. Employees Not Engaged Despite Gains in 2014," Gallup, January 28, 2015, last accessed January 19, 2016, http://www.gallup.com/poll/181289/majority–employees–not–engaged–despite–gains–2014.aspx

18. "2013 Edelman Trust Barometer Executive Summary," last accessed January 19, 2016. http://content.presspage.com/uploads/198/edelmantrustbarometer2013–executivesummary.pdf

19. "The Drum Major Instinct," Martin Luther King, Jr. and the Global Freedom Struggle, date last accessed January 19, 2016. http://kingencyclopedia.stanford.edu/encyclopedia/documentsentry/doc_the_drum_major_instinct/

20. "C.J. Dennis," Wikipedia contributors, *Wikipedia, The Free Encyclopedia,* date of last revision January 7, 2016. Last accessed January 19, 2016. https://en.wikipedia.org/w/index.php?title=C._J._Dennis&oldid=698745350. Primary contributors: Revision history statistics. Page version ID: 698745350.

21. "Robert W. Service," Wikipedia contributors, *Wikipedia, The Free Encyclopedia,* date of last revision December 22, 2015. Last accessed January 19, 2016. https://en.wikipedia.org/w/index.php?title=Robert_W._Service&oldid=696283722. Primary contributors: Revision history statistics. Page version ID: 696283722.

22. Robert Whipple, "Leaders: Hold Yourself Accountable," The Trust Ambassador, April 29, 2012, last accessed January 19, 2016. http://thetrustambassador.com/2012/04/29/leaders-hold-yourself-accountable/

23. "Victor Frankl," Wikipedia contributors, *Wikipedia, The Free Encyclopedia,* date of last revision December 25, 2015. Last accessed January 19, 2016. https://en.wikipedia.org/w/index.php?title=Viktor_Frankl&oldid=696748948. Primary contributors: Revision history statistics. Page version ID: 696748948.

24. Angus Deaton, *The Great Escape: Health, Wealth, and the Origins of Income Inequality;* Princeton University Press; 2015; page 167.

25. "New Deal," Wikipedia contributors, *Wikipedia, The Free Encyclopedia,* date of last revision January 19, 2016. Last accessed January 19, 2016. https://en.wikipedia.org/w/index.php?title=New_Deal&oldid=700603225. Primary contributors: Revision history statistics. Page version ID: 700603225.

26. "Haiku," Wikipedia contributors, *Wikipedia, The Free Encyclopedia,* date of last revision January 19, 2016. Last accessed January 19, 2016. https://en.wikipedia.org/w/index.php?title=Haiku&oldid=700373862. Primary contributors: Revision history statistics. Page version ID: 700373862.

27. "Battle of Agincourt," Wikipedia contributors, *Wikipedia, The Free Encyclopedia,* date of last revision January 19, 2016. Last accessed January 19, 2016. https://en.wikipedia.org/w/index.php?title=Battle_of_Agincourt&oldid=700539743. Primary contributors: Revision history statistics. Page version ID: 700539743.

28. While often attributed to The Elders of the Hopi Nation in Arizona, the Hopi Nation is unable to confirm the source. Also sometimes attributed to the Chumash, Iroquois, Arapaho, and Muscogee tribes. "We are the ones we have been waiting for" variously attributed to Marianne Williamson or June Jordan from a "Poem for South African Women." The verses quoted here are likely a compilation from various authors.

29. Richard Barrett, "Trusting Your Soul to Produce the Outcome that is Most Beneficial to You," Inner Self, 2012. Last accessed January 19, 2016. http://innerself.com/content/personal/attitudes-transformed/fear-and-worry/10800-trusting-your-soul.html

30. "Charge of the Light Brigade," Wikipedia contributors, *Wikipedia, The Free Encyclopedia,* date of last revision January 2, 2016. Last accessed January 19, 2016. https://en.wikipedia.org/w/index.php?title=Charge_of_the_Light_Brigade&oldid=69787083. Primary contributors: Revision history statistics. Page version ID: 697870834.

31. "A Course in Miracles," Wikipedia contributors, *Wikipedia, The Free Encyclopedia,* date of last revision January 15, 2016. Last accessed January 19, 2016. https://en.wikipedia.org/w/index.php?title=A_Course_in_Miracles&oldid=699974655. Primary contributors: Revision history statistics. Page version ID: 699974655.

32. "Flow (psychology)," Wikipedia contributors, *Wikipedia, The Free Encyclopedia,* date of last revision January 7, 2016. Last accessed January 19, 2016. https://en.wikipedia.org/w/index.php?title=Flow_(psychology)&oldid=698670019. Primary contributors: Revision history statistics. Page version ID: 698670019.

33. "Battle of Gettysburg," Wikipedia contributors, *Wikipedia, The Free Encyclopedia,* date of last revision January 15, 2016. Last accessed January 19, 2016. https://en.wikipedia.org/w/index.php?title=Battle_of_Gettysburg&oldid=699958470. Primary contributors: Revision history statistics. Page version ID: 699958470.

34. "Gautama Buddha," Wikipedia contributors, *Wikipedia, The Free Encyclopedia,* date of last revision January 19, 2016. Last accessed January 19, 2016.https://en.wikipedia.org/w/index.php?title=Gautama_Buddha&oldid=700520767. Primary contributors: Revision history statistics. Page version ID 700520767.

35. "In Flanders Fields," Wikipedia contributors, *Wikipedia, The Free Encyclopedia,* date of last revision December 19, 2015. Last accessed January 19, 2016. https://en.wikipedia.org/w/index.php?title=In_Flanders_Fields&oldid=695846404. Primary contributors: Revision history statistics. Page version ID 695846404.

36. "Remarks by Susan B. Anthony in the Circuit Court of the United States for the Northern District of New York," The Elizabeth Cady Stanton & Susan B. Anthony Papers Project. Last accessed January 19, 2016. http://ecssba.rutgers.edu/docs/sba-trial.html

37. "Kahlil Gibran," Wikipedia contributors, *Wikipedia, The Free Encyclopedia,* date of last revision January 11, 2016. Last accessed January 19, 2016. https://en.wikipedia.org/w/index.php?title=Kahlil_Gibran&oldid=699284637. Primary contributors: Revision history statistics. Page version ID 699284637.

38. "Stanford Prison Experiment," Wikipedia contributors, *Wikipedia, The Free Encyclopedia,* date of last revision January 17, 2015. Last accessed January 19, 2016. https://en.wikipedia.org/w/index.php?title=Stanford_prison_experiment&oldid=700198597. Primary contributors: Revision history statistics. Page version ID 700198597.

COPYRIGHT PERMISSIONS

ACKNOWLEDGEMENTS

Writing this book, like good leadership, has been a collaborative effort where many people made contributions large and small. To all of them, I am deeply appreciative.

Many family members listened to my thoughts, read drafts of the manuscript, provided good counsel, offered ideas for new poems to cite, helped research copyright permissions, tracked down authors and publishers, and gave their unflagging support. These include my dear wife, June, our sons, Scott, who helped with copyright permissions, Gregg, who often provided invaluable insights and suggestions, and our niece Dr. Jeanne Kuhajek, who assisted with securing copyright permissions.

Many colleagues and friends reviewed drafts and offered helpful suggestions and/or testimonials including Lori Ames, John Balkcom, Richard Barrett, Karl Bauer, John Blakey, Jack Bogle, Jack Chain, Dick Chandler, Eric Chester, Stephen M. R. Covey, Mike Critelli, Larry Donnithorne, Patricia Fripp, Walt Hampton, Frances Hesselbein, John Horan-Kates, Barbara Brooks Kimmel, Jack Krol, Richard Leider, Marty Linsky, Richard Leider, Bryan Mattimore, Sarah Smith-Orr, Richard Rierson, Frank Sonnenberg, Dan Sweeney, Nancy Tuor Moore, Charlie Walsh, and Bob Whipple. My copyright attorney, Jeff Furr, was instrumental in ensuring we secured all the necessary copyright permissions from the authors and publishers we quoted.

Jim Kouzes and Barry Posner were so much more than kind when they took time to write the Foreword, especially since they were busy getting their own next book into print. Their contributions to the leadership literature over the years has been immense, and I am humbled by their support of my work.

Colleagues whom I had the honor to work with over the years, either quoted or not mentioned by name, were more a part of what I learned about leadership than any formal education I ever received. They were patient with me and often had the courage to tell me when I was off track. To them, I am eternally grateful.

Leadership experts whom I admire have provided much of my ongoing education on this elusive subject of leadership. The list includes Richard Barrett, Warren Bennis, Jim Collins, Stephen Covey, Stephen M.R. Covey, Peter Drucker, Bill George, Robert Greenleaf, Ron Heifitz, Frances Hesselbein, John Horan-Kates, Jim Kouzes, Richard Leider, Marty Linsky, James O'Toole, Barry Posner, Bob Whipple, and more.

Justin Sachs, the CEO at Motivational Press, my publisher, was always supportive and responsive to all my requests and questions, as were Tom Matkovic and Joseph Emnace.

Thank you, all.

INDEX

U

AUTHOR'S BIO

Bob Vanourek is the former CEO of five firms, ranging from a start-up to a $1 billion NY stock exchange company and including winners of a state-level Malcolm Baldrige Quality Award and the Shingo Prize for Operational Excellence shortly after he left.

He and his son Gregg co-authored *Triple Crown Leadership: Building Excellent, Ethical, and Enduring Organizations*, a 2013 USA Best Book Awards Winner. It was called "the best leadership book since *Good to Great.*"

Bob has been a contributing writer to many publications and a chapter contributor to numerous books on ethics, trust, and servant leadership including *Trust Inc.* Volumes 1, 2, and 3, published by Next Decade Inc., 2013, 2014, and 2015; *Reflections on Leadership* (John Wiley and Sons; 1995); *Good Business*, Routledge; 2009; and *Imagine 30 Days to a New You,* Motivational Press, 2016.

Bob is a former adjunct leadership instructor at the University of Denver and Colorado Mountain College. He was Chairman of the Vail Leadership Institute (now a part of the Vail Centre), and a former board member of ten for-profit and non-profit boards. Bob has been a consultant-coach for many corporations, non-profits, and international, state, and local governments.

He is a Baker Scholar graduate (top 5 percent) of the Harvard Business School, a magna cum laude graduate of Princeton University, and a certified leadership instructor from Harvard's Kennedy School of Government and the Phi Theta Kappa Society.

Bob has been named one of the Top Thought Leaders in Trust for 2013–2016, as well as one of the American Management Association's "Leaders to Watch in 2015." Bob is a decorated Army officer and a lifelong student of leadership.

CPSIA information can be obtained
at www.ICGtesting.com
Printed in the USA
FSOW04n1728060516
20174FS